John Williams

An Apology for the Pulpits

being in Answer to a Late Book

John Williams

An Apology for the Pulpits
being in Answer to a Late Book

ISBN/EAN: 9783743378025

Manufactured in Europe, USA, Canada, Australia, Japa

Cover: Foto ©Andreas Hilbeck / pixelio.de

Manufactured and distributed by brebook publishing software
(www.brebook.com)

John Williams

An Apology for the Pulpits

AN
APOLOGY
FOR THE
PULPITS:

Being in

ANSWER

To a late Book, Intituled,

Good Advice to the Pulpits.

Together with an APPENDIX, containing a Defence of Dr. *Tenison*'s Sermon about Alms; in a Letter to the Author of this Apology.

IMPRIMATUR,

Liber cui Titulus, [*An Apology for the Pulpits*, &c. *cum Appendice.*]

Jan. 12. 1687.   H. Maurice, Rmo. in Christo P. D. Wilhelmo Archiep. Cant. a Sacris.

LONDON:

Printed for *Dorman Newman*, at the *Kings-Arms* in the *Poultrey*, MDCLXXXVIII.

A N
A P O L O G Y
FOR THE
P U L P I T S:
I N
A N S W E R
TO THE
Good Advice to the P U L P I T S.

W E have been of late fo much wonted to an Artifice which a fort of men amongft us have taken up, and fo frequently warned of it, that none can now be well deceived, but thofe that are willing to be deceived: For by that time the Reader has but perufed a Page or Two of their Writings, it will be hard if he doth not difcover that the Title and the Defign of the Book are two different things. After this manner proceeds the Author of the *Good Advice to the Pulpits,* who pretends to *deli-* ver *a few Cautions, in which all Pulpits, whether of Con-* formifts,

A 2

formiſts, or *Diſſenters*, *of what ſort ſoever*, *whether Prote-ſtant or Papiſt*, *are concerned* ; as if he would deal his *Ad-vice* with an impartial hand, and from each would have given ſuch Inſtances of their Miſrepreſentations and Falſifications, Errors and Abuſes, as might have been wor-thy of his Caſtigation. But whatſoever he pretends, this is apparently the fartheſt off from his intention ; for he no ſooner enters upon his Task, but he lets drop two parts of his Diſtribution, and excepts the Papiſt and Proteſtant Diſſenter out of the number of thoſe he prepared his Cautions for, and both the Church of *En-gland* and Diſſenter out of the number of thoſe he in-tends to vindicate from the Aſperſions and Abuſes of a

Pag. 2.

Common Adverſary. For thus he begins, *The matter is of Concern*, *and therefore 'twill not be improper to elucidate it by example* ; *and becauſe the Averſion againſt thoſe cal-led Papiſts is moſt general*, *I'le let them be the Inſtance*,

Pag. 1.

that is, of being *blackned with infamous Crimes* ; and if he had added, *becauſe theſe called Papiſts have the great-*eſt *Averſion* againſt the Clergy of the Church of *Eng-land*, *I'le on the other ſide let them be the inſtance* of ha-ving dealt *foully* with them, it had been the juſt interpre-tation of his mind, but would have had in it more in-genuity and fair dealing than we may expect from one of his ſtrain. So that in concluſion, the *Cautions* that he pretends to give to the Pulpits, are but as ſo many Inve-ctives againſt the Pulpits of the Church of *England* ; and the whole deſign of his *Advice* from the beginning to the end of it, is to incenſe the Government of the Nation, and to inſtill into the minds of the peo-ple, prejudices againſt the Clergy of the Eſtabliſhed Church. A Deſign miſchievous enough, but the way he has taken for it is as impertinent as one could wiſh. For who that conſiders the time that our Soveraign has

Reigned,

Reigned, and can tell ten, but can easily underſtand how abſurd and fallacious it is to charge the Pulpits with making their *Prince's Religion odious and contemptible to his Subjects, and thereby to undervalue the Prince to his People*; when the Sermons he quotes for it were preached, ſome of them 20 years ſince, and the reſt in the years 78, 79, 80. How doth he inveigh againſt the Preachers? How Tragical are his Repreſentations? What a bundle has he produced of Accuſations? What diſmal Inferences doth he make from them? Firſt of all, *It does not look like the part of a good Subject, to undervalue his Prince to his own People.* Very well! *And yet he that inveighs againſt his Religion, ſeems to do ſo.* As how, and when! If you would know it, in the years 78, 79, 80. *Such and ſuch Points of his Faith are painted out as Ridiculous, Nonſenſe, Prophane,* &c. And then he wiſely infers, *Are not all theſe ſevere Reflections upon his* [S. M's] *Senſe, his Judgment and Reaſon?* Theſe are Fetches and *Innuendo's*, that are as peculiar and ſurpriſing, as the Inference is indecent and unmannerly. Surely theſe People think there is no Senſe among Mankind, that put ſuch hard things upon them; and others will think there is not much Reſpect to Majeſty, that, when they want Reaſon for their own Vindication, they are preſently lodging their Caſe at their Soveraign's feet; nay, thruſting themſelves and all their Infirmities into his Boſom. Let them behave themſelves like fair Diſputants, and challenge the Sermons with Principles of Diſloyalty to their Prince, or with Diſhoneſty in their Evidences, or Weakneſs in their Arguments. Do they find there the Doctrines of the Peoples Power over Princes, of the Lawfulneſs of Reſiſting, or of a foreign Juriſdiction over their Soveraign? Or rather, where have the Rights of Princes, and the Subjection and Obedience of the People in all lawful

Caſes,

Cases, and the Non-refiftance in any cafe been fo much afferted? A *Teft* that deferves for fome Reasons well known to the World, better *to be wrote over the Pulpits* both of Papift and Diffenter, than that which he would have *a ftanding Teft* for the Preachers. And if this was the Doctrine taught in our Pulpits, whatever they were for Preachers (it's our Author's grievance, I perceive, they are fo good) I am fure they were none of the worft Subjects. But after all, I have fome reason to queftion what *Teft* would fute our Author's Inclinations, who (befides what he difallows of preaching Non-refiftance to the People, *p.* 69.) after all the Advice and Cautions he gives to the Pulpits, has taken no manner of care to lay down any one, about that kind of Loyalty which concerns all, of all Perfwafions, and is taught in the Pulpits of the Church of *England*, which obliges them to be as Loyal when the Prince is of a different Religion, as when he is of the fame with them.

But it's time to come to his Cautions, and to fee how he quits himfelf in that undertaking.

Firft Caution.

THe Sum of this Caution is, That falfe Accufations againft the Innocent get not up into the Pulpit. *Suppofe*, faith he, *that they* [Papifts] *were accufed by men of Infamous Lives, of the worft of Crimes, of defigning againft the Life of their Soveraign, againft the Religion eftablifhed by Law, againft the Liberty and Property of their Fellow-fubjects.* To this he adjoyns his Inftances, and fills up ten Pages with Quotations from feveral Sermons preached in the years 1678, 79, 80. for the moft

part

part before the Lords and Commons affembled in Parliament, and by Perfons of no lefs Character than *A. B. B.* and other dignified Perfons in the Church. Thefe he charges with *fquaring the Gofpel to the fupport and proof* p. 13, &c. *of Calumnies,* that by thus *holding forth,* are a *Scandal to their Profeffion,* that *incited Judges againft the Defendants at the Bar, ftirring up their Gall, and embittering their Spirits, filling the Judges and Lawgivers with Fury and Vengeance, fearing thefe would be too meek and merciful, unlefs fome Clergy-cruelty were inftill'd into them out of the Pulpits.* It is not worth the while to tranfcribe this fort of Flowers, which this Gentleman has, I perceive, a *Copia* of by him: had I a mind, I could eafily recriminate, and remind him by whofe inftigation the *Marian* Flames were formerly kindled in this Nation, and by whom *the Complaint* was made in our neighbouring Nation that led the way to the feverity therein practifed. For the Cafe before us, our Author has fo put it, as no peaceable man can delight to fay much upon it, though it were in his own Vindication; and which he has fo put, as if he did intend to revive thefe *fears and jealoufies* which he pretends to warn us of. For if the *Mobile* are apt (as he faith) p. 15. to *Take Fire at every Flafh,* he muft needs be fenfible that they cannot read fuch Quotations as he produceth, without as well remembring at whofe Order, and before whom they were Preached, as the quality of the perfons that were the Preachers. If the charge was true, then by his own Confeffion, they *were the worft of Crimes,* and whatever the Preachers faid was not to *ftir up the Magiftrates againft Defendants,* but to do Juftice upon Malefactors, and to fecure their Auditors againft fuch mifchievous principles as they were fuppofed to act upon. But becaufe this is not to be fuppofed; if the charge was falfe, and the Pulpits err'd in their Opinion about it;

they

they err'd with thoſe before whom they Preached, and from whom they received their Informations, and by whom they were ordered to Preach upon that occaſion. They err'd with what our Author calls, *The greateſt Tribunal of the Nation* in Parliament ; with *the higheſt and nobleſt Court in this, or perhaps any other part of the Chriſtian World,* as the chief Arbitrator in it, deſervedly calls it : Nay, with their Royal Maſter himſelf, who had ſo often in his Proclamations owned it to the World, and from which the Preachers both took the Information, and very often the Forms of words they choſe to expreſs themſelves in. And after all the *Clergy-cruelty* he ſpeaks of, theſe were the perſons then charged with being cool in it, that were backward to believe it, that were Papiſts in Maſquerade, becauſe they would not run along with that Party that took into their hands the management of that matter. Surely our Author either was not aware of this, or preſumed too much that others were not. If he was not, he has the more need to ſet it down in a *NB.* at the head of his Common-place Book, as a Caution to himſelf, that if for the future he ſhall have occaſion to make uſe of ſuch Quotations, he be careful to conceal the Auditory they were delivered before, as well as the Circumſtances they were in ; leſt he gives too much Authority to the Caſe he would confute, and that the people who he ſaith, are *credulous at the noiſe of Plots and Deſigns,* ſhould be inclined to believe them before himſelf. And if this ſhould happen to be the event, let him aſſure himſelf, whatever allowance he may have from his immediate Superiors for ſuch Publications; he neither deſerves, nor will have any thanks for it from thoſe whoſe deſire and ſtudy it is to be quiet.

P. 18.

Procl. 'Oct. 251. Nul. 17, &c. 1678.

P. 69.

Second

Second Caution.

THE sum of that is, that *if Preachers at any time lay open the Crimes of any People to their Auditory, they be careful not to urge their Accusations farther than they are certain, and know them to be true.*

I hope our Author means not that sort of certainty which they call Infallibility; and that a Preacher must at no time, whatever the occasion be, produce any testimony but what is of that kind. For then what will become of those Miracles of the *great Xaverius* (as one calls him) which he did not onely equal, but exceed our Saviour and the Apostles in, when he is said to raise 25 Persons from death to life. What of the Attestation of Eye-witnesses, and even the *very rigorous Examen?* What of the Anniversary Sermons upon his Festival? Nay, what of the Canonization it self, which we are told is subject to Error? See Assert. 7.

If he comes to a lower certainty, then let him consult not the Preachers, but the Authorities they went upon. As to the last of his Instances under this Caution, *viz. That Jesuits in disguise insinuate themselves among Dissenters,* I will recommend to him *the false Jew,* printed 1653. *the Quaker unmask'd,* and *the New Discovery,* printed 1656. or (because it may be easier procured) the Book call'd *Foxes and Firebrands;* which I must confess I know not what, but he may have more than I know of, to reply to.

Remarks of A. P. upon Dr. Tenison's Narrat. p. 12.

B *Third*

Third Caution

IS, " That the Preacher would not be ſo paſſionately " earneſt in the diſcouraging the People from going " over to another Communion, as to forget both Hone- " ſty, Juſtice, Truth and Charity. That they deſcribe " not the Doctrine of a Church from private Authors, " from the extravagance of ſome Profeſſors. That they " give not out their own wreſted Interpretations, horrid " Miſconſtructions, as the Faith of the Church; eſpeci- " ally that they give not too much Rope to their Infer- " ring Faculty.

This is the ſum of his Third Caution; and here he writes like a Cautious Perſon, and as one ſenſible that without prevention and a timely reſerve, he may meet with ſome diſadvantage, and lay himſelf open to his Ad- verſary. The matters before were Political, he knew he was ſafe : but now he comes to points of Doctrine and matters of Fact in the Church, the old relief is call'd in : perhaps the Preachers did not talk without book, and that if call'd upon, they are able to produce their Authorities, and to juſtify what they ſay by their own Authors that have ſaid it ; and therefore he takes to a ſhelter betimes, that if the ſtorm fall, he may be ſafe. It's either the *Doctrine of private Authors*, or ſome Per- ſons *Extravagance* of their Church ; or elſe it's the Prea- chers *wreſted Interpretations*, or *horrid Miſconſtructions*, and a *giving too much Rope to their Inferring Faculty*. And to repreſent and demonſtrate this, he has collected 27 Pages of Quotations from ſeveral Sermons ; which are,

P. 49. he ſaith, *a ſevere Reflection upon their Reputation*, *upon their Charity*, *upon their Prudence*, *upon their Sincerity*,
with

with moft Sober and Thinking Men. Sober and Thinking
Men ufe not to pafs Judgment without good reafon, and
it may be fuppofed will be ready to ask for what reafon
he fhould thus pafs Judgment for them. To that he is
provided to give an anfwer. Here are *Invectives and
Satyrs inftead of Sermons*——— *Heat and Paffion, Choler*   P. 51.
and Gall——— *prophane Scurrility, unmannerly Jeers, fpite-
ful Exaggerations, groundlefs Inferences, unworthy Charges, empty Sophiftry,* &c. *and fuch Arguments as require a
Fiend at the Elbow.* Whence is all this ? Is that a Vertue in themfelves which is a Vice in others ? And may
one man be wrathful and outragious with Reputation,
whilft another lofes his Reputation by it ? Or may he
that would oblige the Pulpit to a Decorum, obferve none
with his Pen, and by affuming authority to correct a
fault in another, may he challenge a liberty to commit
it ? Affuredly, if the other be *a character-making unwor-*   P. 51.
thy of thofe who profefs a Reformation, this is one that
ftands in need of it : And becaufe he tells us, that to con-
trive it fo as to *let the Teachers teach themfelves, is not* Epift. to R.
fo obnoxious to cenfure ; let him learn better from his own
Maxime ; that *'tis very ridiculous to fee a man doing the*   P. 52.
very thing he condemns. But what is it that has put this
Meek and Moderate, and Peaceable Man, fo much out of
humour, that in the heat of his paffion he fhould thus
confound and contradict himfelf? Blame him not, for it
is for *Religion* that he is fo much concerned.

Be it fo. May not, however, fomewhat be indulged to
their zeal againft his Religion, as well as to his againft
theirs ? But theirs is *a Pulpit-cheat, than which none is*   P.
worfe.

There are *Calumnies, Falfities, Falfe Inferences, Half-
Defcriptions,* &c. And then he throws out a Challenge.

" If

" If the Papists Religion be judged to be Falſe and Er-
" roneous, the way to ſhew it would be to produce their
" Avow'd and Receiv'd Doctrines, and prove them
" to be contrary to Scripture, and to the practice of the
" Primitive Church; this done without Paſſion and In-
" direct means, would not be unjuſt, nor ſo offenſive :
" but why ſhould falſe Things, and ſuch Doctrines as
" they diſavow, be laid to their charge?

Fairly moved! But it's one thing to prove a Doctrine
to be Falſe, another to prove it to be Theirs. The firſt
is to be done by Scripture and Reaſon, and the Primitive
Church, and doth not concern the preſent debate ; and
indeed has been already ſo effectually done, that it will
coſt more time to anſwer it, than to write *A Good Advice.* The latter depends upon Authority ; and ſo whether they are their Doctrines, or whether they diſavow
them, muſt be conſidered from the approved Writers of
their Church. And how far this alſo has been made
good againſt all their late endeavours to palliate, diſ-
guiſe and conceal their Opinions, to the coſt of the thing
call'd *Miſrepreſentation* and *Expoſition*, I leave to the
World to judge, and themſelves to diſprove. A way
that they would never have taken, nor have thus whi-
ned, complain'd and crouched, and have come to
Accommodations and *Agreements*, if they could have bore
up againſt their Adverſaries by Scripture, Reaſon or
Antiquity. But becauſe this at preſent is a Track that
they are in, and, for ought I perceive, cannot go far out
of it, we are willing to follow them, and to hear their
Complaints ; which he has drawn up in 28 Particulars,
extracted from the foregoing Sermons ; and concludes,
*'Tis certain the Papiſts diſown theſe Doctrines, and preach
againſt them as much as thoſe very Doctors who appear ſo
zealous to condemn them. If the Repreſenter had but read*

P. 53.
P. 55.

ſuch

such Sermons as these, he needed not to have look'd further, to have made good his charge of Misrepresenting.

Had I now a mind to bring these Preachers off in the *Adviser's* way, I need but say *they are the opinions of private Authors, the extravagances of some Professors,* and the business would be at an end.

But as the Representer will never be dead so long as our Author is alive; so I shall try whether he is any whit more Infallible and Invincible than the other, by enquiring into those *Doctrines* which, he saith, the Preachers taught, and *positively charge* upon their Church, and their Church *disavows;* and whether he will abide by it that *the Papists preach against them as much as those very Doctors who condemn them.*

To begin then, he saith *it's positively asserted,*

That *the different Orders amongst them* [of the Church Affer. 1. of *Rome*]*are so many Sects, and nothing but Fanaticks pack'd up in Convents.* I have learn'd to wonder at nothing, or else I should, that our Author, who just before exclaims against *horrid Misconstructions,* should at his first setting out be himself so guilty of it, as to change the Terms of what he saith is *positively asserted,* that when the Preacher had said *there are Fanaticks in their Convents,* he makes him to say, there *is nothing but Fanaticks in them.* Let him turn to the words as he quotes them before, and either learn more sincerity, or give less *Rope to his Inferring Faculty,* before he again writes *Cau-* P. 31. *tions* against *wrested Interpretations* and *Misconstructions.* But I shall not thus leave the point. For I acknowledg that there are three things asserted by the Preacher.

1. That the different Orders of Religion among them are so many Sects of Religion.

2. That there are Fanaticks in their Convents.

3. That

3. That to pack up, or diſpoſe of them there, is an advantage that their Church makes of it.

Now let us try what ground there is for them.

1. That *their Orders are ſo many Sects*, that is, ſo many diſtinct Bodies, that having different Founders, Rules, Habits, and often Opinions, by which an Emulation is begot betwixt Order and Order, they become divided among themſelves ; and when occaſion is offer'd, do actually war one upon another in their way. It would be an endleſs task to travel through this Argument, and to give an Hiſtorical Relation of the Feuds that have been among them, and have ſometimes for ſeveral Ages together moleſted their Church. Such was the Controverſie about the ſize of their Hoods, and which, after an Age ſpent in the debate, was difficultly managed and ended by the Four Popes, during whoſe Reign it continued. Such again was that of the *Immaculate Conception of the Virgin Mary*, which was defended by the *Franciſcans*, and oppoſed by the *Dominicans*, and which continued for 300 years together, having engaged Popes, Princes, Biſhops, Univerſites, and whole Nations in it, ſuch as *France, Spain, Italy, Germany*, and is not yet ended *.

* *Lucas Wadding.* Legatio de Concept. Sect. 3. Tract. 12.

Such again were thoſe Diſſentions betwixt the *Jeſuits* and *Dominicans* in the time of *Clement* VIII. and *Paul* V †.

† *S. Amour Journal.*

Such are thoſe between the *Franciſcans* and the *Jeſuits*, which have ſometimes been ſo great and fierce, that each has proceeded to the Excommunication of the other ‖.

‖ V. Excommunication publiſhed by *Tho. Flemming,* A. B. of *Doublin,* Anſwered, &c. *An.* 1633. p 19.

So that it is no wonder we find men of Learning and Experience complaining of it frequently among themſelves. Thus *Lucas Wadding* ſaith in his Hiſtory above mentioned, that he dares not relate fully what happen'd upon the Contention about the *Immaculate Conception,* becauſe of the Scandals of it.

2. *There*

2. *There are Fanaticks in their Convents. Fanaticifm* is a general name, and comprehends in it Superftition and Enthufiafm. The Former is the placing Religion in thofe things which Religion is not concerned in. The Latter is when perfons are acted and governed by fome fuppofed Communications from Heaven, by Revelations, Vifions, Infpirations, by Raptures and Illuminations, and unaccountable Impulfes. Of the former fort are their Orders themfelves, their Habits and Rules, and the Priviledges granted to them, and depended upon ; of which more hereafter : and which indeed very much arife from the latter. For to that [Enthufiafm] we owe the Orders and their Inftitution. So *Bellarmin* faith, That *the Orders of* De Pont Rom. *St.* Benedict, *St.* Romoaldus, *St.* Bruno, *St.* Dominick, l. 3. c. 18. *St.* Francis, *were at firft inftituted by the Infpiration of the Holy Ghoft.* And St. *Brigit* faith, the Rules of the feve- Brigitt. Reve-ral Orders in her time *were all received from him.* lat. l. 7. c. 20.

To this they do not a little owe many of their Do- p. 559.
ctrines, fuch as Purgatory, and Tranfubftantiation, and Bellarm. de
the Immaculate Conception, &c. And many of the Purg. l. 1. c. 11.
things defined and obferved in their Church ; as Sacra- De Sacram.
ments, Feftivals and Canonizations, &c. Euch. l. 3. c. 8.
                                                          Wadding Le-
And yet we have great reafon to queftion thefe Re- gat. de con-
velations, &c. not only becaufe it derogates from the au- cept. V. M.
thority of Divine Revelation, but alfo becaufe they are Sect. 3. n. 41.
far from agreeing in thefe matters among themfelves. p. 371.
And of this I fhall produce an inftance beyond all exception.

It is the cafe above mentioned, about *the Immaculate Conception*, in which we have Revelation againft Reve-lation, Saint againft Saint, Order againft Order, and Pope againft Pope. For it are produced the Revelations v. *Wadding* of St. *Brigit*, which after a diligent enquiry by her Con- Legatio & Dr. feffors, and by Bifhops in her own Country, *Sweden*, Still. Fanat. of the Ch. of R. were p. 244, &c.

were approved of; and from thence tranfmitted at laft to *Rome*; where by the appointment of two or three feveral Popes fucceffively, the Teftimonies were examined by Commiffioners; and all confirmed by the Council of *Bafil*; and fhe Canonized by *Boniface* the Ninth. And if this was not a *very rigorous examen*, I fhould diftruft even that of *A. P*'s, concerning his *great Xaverius*. And yet after all comes St. *Catharine* of *Siena*, with her Revelations to the contrary, who was Canonized by *Pius 2d.* and is faid by him in his Bull to be *divinely infpired*, and her *Extafies* are declared to be *Holy* in the publick Offices of their Church, no lefs than thofe of St. *Brigit*. What fhall we fay in this Cafe? Nay, what is faid by themfelves? They e'ne fay as they are for or againft the *Immaculate Conception*: Thofe that are for it, charge the others with Forgery, as *Delrio* doth the *Dominicans*. Thofe that are againft it, call the Revelations of the other, *Fantaftic Vifions*, and *Old Wives Dreams*, as do *Antoninus* (now a Canonized Saint) and *Cajetan*; let Popes and Breviaries fay what they will. And thofe that are concerned in neither, will think hardly enough of both; and if they call it by the fofter name of Enthufiafm and Fanaticifm (in which their Cloyfters do abound) they are more civil to both, than either of themfelves is to the other.

3. However let it be as it will, the Church of *Rome* makes a fingular *advantage* of it, and artificially prevents the mifchief that might arife from it. For thereby not only countenance is given to many of her Doctrines and Practices; but alfo it being *brought* (as the Preacher faith) *under fome kind of Rule and Government*, it's like Fire in a Chymical Furnace, that the Artift by his Regifters applies and directs as he has ufe and occafion for it: And if at any time it happens to be rampant and

and outragious, yet it being ſhut up in a Cloyſter, as Fire in *Ætna*, it then ſpends it ſelf for the moſt part (tho' ſometimes it has happened otherwiſe, and which the moſt politick conſtitution cannot wholly prevent) without doing that miſchief it would produce if at large and left entirely to it ſelf. This is the grave account Mr. *Creſſy* gives of this matter ; *If they have new and ſtrange Revelations, they are not ſeditious and troubleſom to the World* [except as before excepted]——*becauſe theſe are enjoyed in ſolitude and retirement ; and ſuppoſing they be miſtaken, no harm would accrew to others by it.* Sometimes indeed *harm* has *accrewed* (as in the tumults about the Immaculate Conception) but more often *Advantage*; or elſe they had never been ſo much cheriſhed and indulged in the Church of *Rome.*

Preface to S *Sophia.* Sect. 33.

The Sacrament with them is a Real, Propitiatory, but not a Repreſentative Sacrifice. And Chriſt's Body is Really broken, and his Blood Actually ſpilt on their Altars.* I perceive our Author has ſo much the *faculty* of what he decries, that he can ſcarcely repeat, and much leſs alter the Words of his Adverſary, but he muſt alter the Senſe : And ſo he doth here; for he makes the Preacher to charge that upon the *Papiſts* as a *poſitive Aſſertion,* which is only a natural Inference from their *Aſſertion.* His words are (as the Adviſer quotes them before) *In the* Roman *Church the Sacrament muſt Now be no longer a Repreſentative, but a Real Propitiatory Sacrifice.* The word *Now* ſhews what the Preacher meant, That ſince the Church of *Rome* makes the Sacrifice of the Maſs to be Real and Propitiatory, the Reaſon of the thing will teach that (whatever they ſay) it cannot be Repreſentative ; it being no more poſſible that what is Real and Propitiatory can be Repreſentative, than what is Repreſentative can be Real and Propitiatory ; for otherwiſe the

Aſſert. 2.

C

thing

thing that already is, is a Repreſentation of it ſelf. Thus it was with the Sacrifice which our Bleſſed Saviour of-fer'd upon the Croſs, that was Real and Propitiatory, and not Repreſentative; and if that in the Maſs be the ſame (as they acknowledg) an Expreſſion hedged in as a _Salvo_, will not make that to be true and reconcilable, which Scripture teaches to be falſe, and Reaſon teaches to be a contradiction in _Adjecto_.

He ſtill goes on in the ſame way of _Miſrepreſenting_, and by leaving out the firſt part of the Sentence, maims the reſt. For thus the Preacher proceeds, joyning what follows to what immediately went before——_And Chriſt's Natural Body muſt be brought down from Heaven upon ·a Thouſand Altars at once, and there really broken, and offered up again to the Father, and his Blood Actually ſpilt a thouſand times every day._

It's apparent by the Connexion, and the _muſt be_, that the Preacher is arguing againſt them upon their own Principles, That if there be a Real and Propitiatory Sa-crifice, and Chriſt's Body and Blood be ſubſtantially there, and that what was offered upon the Croſs is Really and Actually offered upon the Altar, then there muſt be the Body Really broken, and the Blood Actually ſpilt. The Preacher knew well enough that the Church of _Rome_, which holds that there is whole Chriſt bodily under each Species, and under every particle of either, doth alſo hold, that what is broken is not the Body, nor what is ſpilt is not the Blood, but only the Accidents belong-ing to Bread and Wine, without their Subſtance. Now the Preacher could no more underſtand that there ſhould be nothing there but the Body and Blood of Cnriſt, and yet what was broken was not the Body, and what was ſpilt was not the Blood, than he could underſtand how the Accidents of Bread and Wine could be there without
the

the substance of Bread and Wine ; or the Accidents could be broken, where the substance was not present. Something is really broken and spilt, if it be a Real and Propitiatory Sacrifice ; something is really broken and actually spilt, as our senses tell us, and as they acknowledg : And that the Body and Blood should only be there, and yet that not be the body that is broken, nor that be the blood that is spilt, is next to the affirming that its broken and not broken, spilt and not spilt ; grant the Preacher the Reason, and much good may it do them with their Assertion. Now, Where *is the passion*, or where *the indirect means* used by the Preacher? It's indeed plain Reasoning ; and if Reasoning be what our Adviser has so great a spight at under the Names of the *Inferring Faculty*, and *Drawing Consequences*, it may be consistent enough with an Implicit Faith, but not with that the Apostle would have us be able to give a Reason of.

In Transubstantiation they renounce all their five Senses. Assert. 3.
Here our Adviser trips again ; For is there no difference betwixt, *Men must renounce all their five senses*, as the Preacher said ; and *the Papists do renounce all their five senses*, as our Monitor saith ? The former is to shew that men can upon no less Reason embrace Transubstantiation, than the renouncing their Senses : The latter is to say, that they that hold Transubstantiation, do professedly and actually renounce their Senses. The truth of the former depends upon the truth of the Reasoning, and its an Argument drawn *ab absurdo* ; That if sense be a proper judge of sensible objects, and if what my sense tells me is there, the Doctrine of Transubstantiation will not allow to be there, then I cannot be for Transubstantiation, but I must quit the judgment of Sense, and my Sense must so far be no Sense. And what can be Reasoning, if this be not ? or how can I have a better

Argu-

gument against any Principle, than that I muſt renounce
thoſe Principles by which alone I am capable of making
a true judgment upon it? As for the latter, tho' the
Preacher doth not charge it upon them that *they actually
and profeſſedly renounce their Senſes* in Tranſubſtantiation; yet they come not far ſhort of it, if they heark-
en to their Church, which requires their Preachers to
*Catechiſ. ad
Paroch.* teach the people that they careſully abſtract from ſenſe in
this matter, which in plain Engliſh is to lay it aſide.

But all this while, for ought I know, I may be in an Error, and that our Author's Reflection is upon the Phraſe,
All their Five; for I have learn'd of late that there is
one of the Senſes for Tranſubſtantiation : And that
tho' what we *See*, and *Taſt*, and *Feel*, and *Smell*, is Bread
and Wine; yet *Hearing* tells us otherwiſe, which is *the*
A Short Cate. *Senſe Faith challenges*; and you muſt *hear the Church ;*
chiſm by way and the Church tells us it's the fleſhly Body of Chriſt.
of Q and A.
1686. If this be our Author's meaning, I have done with him,
till he can ſhew me a Church that has ſuch an Organical
Tongue to ſpeak, as I have an Ear to hear.

Aſſert. 4.   *That the Pope in his Chair cannot err if he would; and all
others without his Aſſiſtance cannot but err.* This is the firſt
Matter of Doctrine that our Adviſer hath produced from
his Authorities; and ſo indeed the Preacher expreſly calls
the firſt part of it, *The Doctrine of the Pope's Infallibility.*

One would have thought that when our Author is ſo
warm upon this Argument, and vehemently expoſtu-
lates after this manner; *Why ſhould Falſe things, and
ſuch Doctrines as they diſavow be laid to their charge ? Why
ſhould it be ſo poſitively aſſerted in the Pupits, That ——
The Pope in his Chair cannot Err ?* One would have
thought, I ſay, that this is a pure Invention of the
Preacher, a ſpice of his *Inferring Faculty*; and that

its

it's certain the Papifts difown this Doctrine, and Preach against it, as much as thofe very Doctors who appear fo zealous to condemn it. To fay the Truth of it, I find this charged upon the Church of *Rome* in fo many Proteftant Books, that if it be not traced to *Rome*, and found at the *Limina Apoftolorum*, nay, in the *Chair* it felf, I will cry out with him of *Falfities* and *Calumnies*. But I am every day more and more hardned againft *Implicit Faith*; for I plainly perceive that Reprefenting and Mifreprefenting are by ufe made fo much alike, that if things improve this way they are at prefent in, we fh.ll not know whether White be White, and Black Black: And therefore I am for the old way, and fhall try whether what our Author difavows in his Churches Name, the Church it felf and other Authors (as much to be credited) in that Church, do indeed difavow: I fhall begin with Cardinal *Hofius*, who faith, *God requires not that a Man* In *Confefs.* *fhould confider whether the Pope be a* Judas, *or a* Peter, *or* Petricov. c.29. *Paul, but only this, That he fits in* Peter's *Chair——from whofe mouth he is commanded to feek the Law. This thing only would* Chrift *have him to obferve.*

'And again ; *Be the wickednefs of Popes never fo great,* Id l. 2. *it cannot hinder but the Promife of God fhall ever be true,* Contr. Brent. *The Popes fha'l ever fhew thee the truth of Judgment.*

Let us proceed to Cardinal *Bellarmine*, He faith, *That* De Rom. *the Pope, whether he be an Heretick or not, cannot by any* Pontif. l. 4. *means define what is heretical, to be believed by the whole* c. 2. Sect. *Church.* And he adds, *That this is the moft common opi-* tentia. *nion of almoft all Catholicks, and is the moft certain opinion, and to be maintained.* And this he further labours to prove Cap. 3. from Scripture, and produces the Teftimonies of feveral Popes. *Suarez* delivers this almoft in the words of our Preacher; and as he begins with, *This is the Catholick* De triplici *Truth;* fo he concludes, *Thus all the Catholick Doctors* virtue. Theol. *teach* Sect. 8. Difp. 5. de reg p. 21a *teach in theſe days.* It were endleſs to heap up Authorities of this kind, and therefore before the Adviſer comes again to find out Miſrepreſentations in the Sermons of the Church of *England*, and to caution its Preachers, let him firſt teach his own, and clear the Fountain-head, even *Rome* it ſelf, and give the Chair due correction, from whence all this Miſrepreſenting Doctrine is derived; and hath diffuſed it ſelf ſo as to become Catholick, if the foreſaid Author is to be credited.

As for the other branch of the Preacher's Saying, that *all others, without his aſſiſtance, cannot but err,* its joyn'd to *he alone cannot err,* and ſo are oppoſite parts: The firſt is granted by thoſe that ſay the Pope is Infallible, That is, is ſo Infallible, that he *alone* is out of a poſſibility of erring; and conſequently all beſides him are Fallible, that is, are liable to err, and can neither be ſecured againſt it, nor know but that they actually do err without his aſſiſtance and direction. Therefore, ſaith *Bellarmine, The Church doth always want ſome one by whom it may be confirmed, whoſe Faith cannot fail.* If the Preacher went beyond this, what Author or Authors he had for it, I know not; they do not at preſent occur to me. The firſt Branch is the point, and that I queſtion not but I have ſufficiently vindicated him in.

They propheſie in an Unknown Tongue. By which the Adviſer would doubtleſs have the Reader think the Preacher ſo abſurd, as toſay that they of the Church of *Rome* do preach in an Unknown Tongue to the People. I commend his ingenuity here however, that he has retained the Preacher's own Term: but I ſhould have commended it more if he had ſet the whole Sentence again before the Reader's Eye, which is, *She profeſſedly edifies the People in Ignorance by praying and propheſying in an Unknown Tongue.* I deny not but the Apoſtle in 1 *Cor.* 14. calls expounding the
Articles

(marginal notes:)
De R. Pontif. l. 4. c. 3. Sect. Altera.

Aſſert. 5.

Articles of Chriftian Faith, and of the Scriptures that contain it, by the name of *Prophefie*; and that the two branches of his Difcourfe, and in which he fhews the unprofitablenefs and abfurdity of ufing an Unknown Tongue, are Prophefie and Prayer. But yet it doth not appear to me that the Preacher here underftood it of vulgar preaching, becaufe he knew it to be otherwife: and if he had fo meant, he would rather have chofe the Term more known, than that which is lefs; and fince he ufed prophefying and not preaching, its apparent he did not mean preaching by prophefying. But what then did he mean by it? What could he mean but that which he is fpeaking about, The publick Service of that Church? (of which preaching is no part) which confifts of Prayers, and Leffons, (either taken out of the Scriptures or Legends) and Hymns? And whereas the one as well as the other fhould according to the Apoftle's reafoning be in a Known Tongue, for Edification; in the Church of *Rome* the one as well as the other is in a Tongue Unknown to the People; and fo that end is defeated. And when he can prove that the Scriptures are not to be read in the Church, or the Hymns not to be ufed in a Known Tongue, or that thefe are not parts of the Service diftinct from their Prayers, or can fhew us that they are read among them in a Tongue known to the People, it will be time to give him a farther anfwer. But more of this anon.

They make no other ufe of Confeffion than what profefs'd Affert. 6. *Drunkards do of vomiting.*

This Affertion of the Preacher concerns not the Doctrine, but the Practice of the Church; nor the Practice of the Church fo much as many of thof.. that are of it. It's matter of Fact and Obfervation, and fo is to be judged of either by the Confeffion of the Church it felf, or

by

Alvar. Pelarg.
de planct. Eccl.
l. 2. art. 78.
p 255. . by Obſervation. That it is ſo, is paſt contradiction; So faith one of themſelves, ſpeaking of thoſe that come to Confeſſion, *What they ſay one day, that they ſay the next; as if every day they ſinned alike.* But though it be ſo, yet the Church is not chargeable with it, unleſs there be ſuch Doctrines and Penances in the Church as do give not only occaſion, but encouragement to it. The Former I ſhall make good, *Aſſert.* 21. And the Latter is notoriouſly evident, not only from common Experience, but from the Book called *Taxa Cameræ Apoſtolicæ;* in which the Abſolutions are ſet at a price for Crimes of all ſorts; and of which Book *Eſpencæus* (a Learned Bi-

Comment. ad
Tit. c. 1. *Di-*
greſſ. 1. ſhop of theirs) ſaith, that *it's ſo far from being ſuppreſs'd, that the Licenſes and Impunities are for the moſt part continued.*

Aſſert. 7. *Their Saints are Canonized for Treaſons, deteſtable Villanies, as a reward of ſtrife and every evil work.* As our Author has ordered the matter, it looks as if the Preacher had aſſerted that *Treaſon,* &c. was the conſtant, or at leaſt the moſt prevalent reaſon for Canonization in the Church of *Rome;* whereas the words are plainly otherwiſe: For thus the Adviſer himſelf had before ſet them down; *It's much leſs* [lawful to pray] *to thoſe that Have been Canonized for Money or for Treaſon,* &c. All he ſaith is, that ſuch *Have been* Canonized for theſe reaſons; which being matter of Fact, and a charge of Male-adminiſtration, we muſt enquire whether any ſuch Perſons, and upon ſuch motives, have been Canonized in the Church of *Rome.* And in order to this I ſhall ſhew, that according to the Principles of that Church it may ſo happen; and then I ſhall conſider what in Fact has been done.

Upon their Principles it may ſo happen. For it's granted

1. In

1. In general, That the Pope, however Infallible in matters of Faith, is Fallible, and may Err in matters of Fact, and in things depending upon humane Testimony; and that though he takes the Advice of his Councellors, and be in a General Council. This *Bellarmine* saith *all Catholicks agree in.* *De Pontif. Rom l. 4. c. 2. SS. His notatis.*

2. From hence it follows, that Canonization being matter of Fact, and depending upon Testimony, the Pope himself may Err in it. And of this mind are several eminent Men in that Church; *Canus* for one, who saith, that *the Church in it leans upon the Testimony of men, which may deceive, and be deceived.* It's an *Examen,* in *Loc. l. 5. c. 5. qu. 5. concl. 3.* Mr. *P's* phrase; and let the *Examen be very rigorous,* even as great as that in the Case of *Xaverius,* it's an *Examen* still. The Canonizer may therefore be mistaken, and may Canonize a Rebel for a Saint.

Farther, This has been done. In how fair a way it was for it, let the History of *Maria Visitationis,* Abbess of the Annuntiation at *Lisbon,* be an instance; who by having 32 Wounds upon her head made (as she pretended) by our Saviour's putting his Crown of Thorns upon it, and by her great Reputation for Holiness, imposed first of all upon her Confessor, the Learned *Ludovicus Granatensis;* then upon the Inquisition, who examined and approved these Marks; then upon Pope *Gregory* XIII. who encouraged her to go on in the way she had begun; and I need not add, upon whole Nations. If she had died in these Celebrated Circumstances, she that was so like to, nay, that exceeded St. *Francis* in these Sacred Stigmata, had been doubtless enroll'd in the Number of Saints; and had had all the 7 Honours due to such (which *Bellar-* *De Sanct. Beat. l. 1. c. 7. SS. Sed antequam,* *mine* hath recited) conferr'd upon her.

But

Lud. a Para-
mo de Orig.
Inquis, l. 2.
Tit. 2. c. 15.
n. 11, &c.
But this was prevented, for the whole was discovered to be Imposture, and a cunning contrivance to set on foot the Revolt of *Portugal* from *Spain*; and which I question not but King *Philip* gave the name of Treason to.

But this is but a probability, and therefore let us proceed, and come nearer home; and there we have an instance in the famous *Thomas a Becket,* A. B. of *Canterbury*; of whose Rebellion against his Prince our Chronicles treat at large; and of whose Canonization the *Roman* Offices are a sufficient Evidence. And now whether this Adherence of his to the Pope against his Leige Prince was not Treason, or whether it was not an Inducement for his Canonization, let the Law speak for *Breviar. Sa-*
risb. Fest.
S. Tho. Cant. the one, and the Office for his day for the other, where they pray *that God by his Blood would save us, and bring us to Heaven.*

Assert. 8. *They pray to a Crucifix as well as to Christ himself; and attribute as much satisfaction to it as to the Blood of their Redeemer.* The Preacher appeals for this to their Offices, and thither we must go. For this that is here spoken of, being a charge of Words and Forms, we must know whether the Charge be true or false, by considering those Forms. And if words will make it plain, the Preacher was not mistaken. For thus the Bishop prays *Pontif. in Be-*
ned. Nov. Cru-
cis. at the Consecration of a Crucifix, *that God would bless the Wood of the Cross, that it may be a saving Remedy to Mankind, a stedfastness of Faith, an increase of good Works, the Redemption of Souls,* &c. When the Cross is thus Consecrated, and has upon Consecration this Divine Capacity bestow'd upon it, wherein doth it in its vertue differ in words from Christ himself? And why may it not then be pray'd to? And whether it be not so, let the Hymn *Vexilla Regis,* shew, and that part in it so often used, *O Crux ave spes unica,* &c. *Hail O Cross, our Only Hope,*

Hope, increafe grace in the good, and blot out the fins of the guilty. For the expofition and vindication of which, let me commend' our Author for Advice, to his Friend *the Reprefenter and Mifreprefenter;* and with them Inconfultation I fhall alfo leave this Head.

. Confeffion tends to the debauching both Laity and Clergy. Affert. 9. The words of the Preacher (as our Author quotes them before) are, that *particular Confeffion of Sins* to the Prieft *inftead of keeping up a wholfome Difcipline, is the way to corrupt it — when the Confeffer and Penitent begin to difcover and underftand one another.* The Preacher grants Confeffion to be a *wholfome Difcipline,* but as it's maintained and practifed in the Church of *Rome,* where the fecrets of a man's breaft muft be depofited in that of the Prieft, it cannot but often expofe the Confeffor and Confeffed to dangerous fnares. And that he was not herein miftaken, we have many inftances. What the cafe was in the Socrates, *l.* 5. *c.* 19. Church of *Conftantinople,* that all perfons were fet loofe from that obligation of private Confeffion, by *Ne-* Sozom. *l.* 7. *c.* 16. *ctarius,* Predeceffor in that See to S. *Chryfoftom,* I leave to our Authors confideration.

This I am fure of, many wife and good men in the Biel *in Can.* Lect. 77. Church of *Rome* have complained of grofs mifcarriages in *Alv. Pelarg.* their own Church, from whom let our Advifer learn it *Art.* 27. *p.* 11 rather than from me; and to them I refer him. *&c.*

And if this was not, or what was very rarely to be ob- *Opufc.* Cajet. Tract. 22. ferved, why are fuch fhameful Cafes relating to this matter Bull of *Pius* put by their Cafuifts, *Utrum Confeffor, &c?* or why was the IVth to there Bull after Bull from the Pope's *contra folicitantes in* the Bifhop of *Confeffione?* He that will fatisfy himfelf in this, let him *Setil. A. D.* 1561. and of read *Joh. Efcobar a Corro* upon the Bulls of *Pius* IV. to the *Gregory* the Bifhop of *Sevil,* and of *Gregory* XIII. XVth. 1622.

That every thing is meritorious with them that is for the Affert. 10. *Church's Intereft.* The words of the Preacher, are (it

feems

seems) as follows. *The Churches Interest is the Center of their Religion, and their Consciences turn upon the same pin. Every thing is pious, conscientious, and meritorious, that makes for their Cause.* Now if the former part be true, that *the Churches Interest is the Center of their Religion,* then the latter is not to be wonder'd at, that *every thing is meritorious with them that makes for that Interest.* The Former part the Preacher undertakes to prove.

1. From the *Supernumerary Articles of the Council of Trent.*

2. He proves it from their *Politick Creed*, the Articles of which the Preacher tells us are such as these. That *the King is the Pope's or the Peoples Creature,* and may be *deposed* by either of them for *Tyranny* or *Heresie,* &c. How much He is the Peoples Creature, let *Bellarmine* tell him. And how much he is the Pope's, let him learn from seven of their own General Councils; and whether this be not to serve their Interest, let him learn from *Lessius,* who makes the Doctrine of Deposition as necessary *to maintain the Authority of the Church,* as to be received for *an Article of Faith.*

Discussio Decreti Mag. Concil. Later. p. 89.

How far the Preacher enlarged upon the latter part, that *it's meritorious with them,* &c. I know not, (having seen no more of the Sermon than the Adviser is pleased to give us) but I find that once upon a time, those that fought against a prevailing sort of Heretick were esteemed to merit Heaven by it. If our Author desire it, I shall direct him for it to good Authority. But for the present I shall only ask his sense of a certain Passage I have met with; It is this. " It seems to us, that no Consti-

Constit. Societ. Jesu, par. 6. c. 5.

" tutions, Declarations, or any Order of Living can " bring upon [any] an obligation to Mortal or Venial " Sin , unless the Superiour should command those " things in the name of our Lord Jesus Christ, or in
                                                                      " the

" the vertue of Obedience, which may be done in
. " thofe things, and by thofe perfons in which it fhall be
" judged, that it fhall much conduce to the particular
" good of any one, or to the Univerfal good. If I underftand this at all, the *good it may conduce to,* whether
particular or univerfal, will make venial or mortal Sin to
be none ; or which is the fame, will make it lawful to
be done, when *commanded by the Superior.* But of this
again, Affertion the 12*th.*

They change Scripture into Legends, the Sacraments in Affer. 11.
*to Shows, Preach Purgatory inftead of Repentance, and
Faction inftead of Faith.* This is put by way of Suppo-
fition in the Sermon, but yet I acknowledg it's level'd
againft the Church of *Rome,* and by which the Preacher
intended to fet forth fome of the grofs corruptions of it.
The Points are Four.

1. *They change Scripture into Legends* ; That is, either
accounting Legends of as good Authority as Scripture,
or by ufing Legends in their Service inftead of Scripture.
There is too much occafion given for the firft ; and the
fecond is too evident to be denied. By Scripture we
mean that Book which both contains in it matters of
Divine Revelation, and was writ by perfons Divinely infpired.   And fince Divine Revelation gives it its Authority, whatever has that Authority given to it, is made
equal with ·Scripture : For Divine Authority is always
alike. But now there are Legends or Narratives of the
Saints Lives, Miracles and Revelations that are owned
by the Church of *Rome* to be of Divine Revelation ;
And why not then are they of as good Authority as the
·Scripture? I could cloy the Reader with Inftances of this
kind ; But let that of St. *Brigit* ferve, whofe Revelations
they own in their publick Offices, to have *come immedi-* Breviar. Rom.
ately from God to her. In which alfo they often ufe Le- 8. Octob.
gends inftead of Scripture, and have put out Scripture
for

for Legends, as the diſcouragement. of Cardinal *Guig-nonius's* deſign ſhews, whoſe Reformation of the Breviary, and his inſertions of Scripture into inſtead of their Legends, would not be admitted. And yet what the Legends generally are, let us take from an Impartial hand, that of their Learned *Eſpencæus*, who ſaith they are *as full of vanity, as Stables of Dung.*

In 2 Tom Digreſſ. l. 1. c. 11.

    2. *They turn Sacraments into Shows.* And is not this done, when the people are ſhew'd the Cup, but not ſuffer'd to partake of it? When the Prieſt alone doth often Communicate? When the Hoſt is elevated at the Maſs for Adoration, and carried about the Streets in publick Proceſſion? Which are ends the Sacrament was never intended for, nor have we a Syllable about it in Scripture.

    3. *They Preach Purgatory inſtead of Repentance.* The thing ſuppoſed here is, that the Doctrine of Purgatory doth invalidate that of Repentance, and gives encouragement to defer and neglect it.

And that it doth,

    1. As it takes people off from the conſideration of one of the moſt powerful Arguments to Repentance, and that is the Fear of Hell, or Eternal Torment. For if there be a middle ſtate for thoſe that are meanly good, then thoſe that conceive themſelves not to be groſly wicked, comfort themſelves with the hopes of this.

    2. It makes them more ſtudious of what will make them ſafe, than what will make them happy; and if they ſtop at Purgatory, they are not concerned for any thing farther.

    3. It makes them put off their Repentance, ſo far at leaſt as what they call Satisfaction is concerned; becauſe they ſhall have a further allowance of time for it in another ſtate.

    4. And ſo much the rather, as they may there be relieved or delivered from thence by the Maſſes, Prayers and Alms of the Living.   - Now

Now if Purgatory be Preached, we may underſtand how much the Doctrine of Repentance loſes of its weight, authority and obligation thereby. And if they do Preach Purgatory inſtead of Repentance, and preſs one more than the other, there is a reaſon for it which I care not to name; no more than I ſhall endeavour to charge the matter of Fact upon them at preſent.

4. *Inſtead of Faith they Preach up Faction.* The Preacher ſuppoſeth this has been done, and done with acceptance. And ſo far as the Doctrines of the Pope's Juriſdiction over Princes, and his power to depoſe them has been Preached, I ſhould not ſcruple to call it Faction, and by a harder name; tho' what our Author will call it, I know not; but he leaves us to ſuſpect what he would not call it by his omiſſion of the next Clauſe to it:

To be falſe and deceitful, is to become worthy of Heaven. Aſſer. 12. The Preacher after the former Clauſe thus proceeds: *Tho' inſtead of Obedience we became guilty of Treaſon; Nay, ſhould we Murther Princes, and prove falſe and deceitful to mankind, all would be well, and we in an inſtant thought worthy of a better Kingdom.* He muſt not blame us here, if we put him in mind of two of our Nation, and of an Order named by the Preacher, that we find in the Catalogue of their Martyrs, tho' they juſtly ſuffer'd for Treaſon; and which is ſomewhat greater, of the Bibliotheca ſolemn Oration made at *Rome* after the Aſſaſſination of Thuanus Jeſuit. *Henry* 3*d,* and the Character given therein to the wretch Tem. 4. l. 95. that imbrued his hands in that Prince's Blood. An. 1589.

Sometimes with Money they compound for their unfor- Aſſert. 13. *ſaken Sins.* Of this, ſee the Appendix.

If the Pope and his Emiſſaries ſay the Right hand is Aſſert. 14. *the Left, the Papiſts are bound to believe it.* The Preacher refers to a Gloſs of theirs for it, which our Author has fairly left out, and there I might leave
it:

it. But I am willing to enquire further into it. This, how ſtrange foever it may ſeem to *thinking men* (in our Author's Phraſe) yet is very well confiſtent with their Religion, which takes them off from thinking; and with thoſe Principles that lead to it. As to begin with what the Preacher introduces this with, ſaith he,

1. They hold that the Pope is, *Alter Deus in Terra,* *another God upon the Earth*; and if he will have it in other terms, *Dominus Deus noſter Papa, Our Lord God the Pope*; The places are well known in their Gloſſes on the Canon Law, that ſpeak thus reſpectfully of him. Grant the Pope but the thing that theſe Titles belong to, and he may well be allowed the Authority of being believed if he ſhould ſo determine that *the Right hand is the Left.*

2. I may add, That this is no more than what is included in the Doctrine of *Implicit Faith*; by which perſons are obliged to believe the Church, as well when they have no Reaſon, as when they have; in which they are not only *ſafe*, but do what is *meritorious.* That they are *Safe*, ſaith (*a*) Cardinal *Hoſius*; That it's *Meritorious*, ſaith (*b*) Cardinel *Tolet.*

(*a*) Contr. Brent. l. 3. p. 146.
(*b*)De Inſtruct Sacred.l.4.c.3. Sect. 7.
De Rom.Pont. l.4.c.5. SS.ult.

3. If I am not miſtaken, Virtue is the *Right hand* in Morality, and Vice is the *Left*; and yet *Bellarmine* ſaith, *If the Pope ſhould err in commanding Vices, or forbidding Virtues, the Church would be bound to believe Vices to be good, and Virtues to be evil, unleſs ſhe would ſin againſt Conſcience.* And I think the Rule of *Ignatius* given to his Society, imports no leſs, That if *the Catholick Church defines that to be Black, which appears to them to be White, they are notwithſtanding to account it to be Black.*

Ignatii Exerc. Spirit.Reg.13.

4. Its brought ſtill lower; For thoſe of *Ignatius*'s Order are to *renounce not only their own wills, but their underſtandings alſo, without calling any thing into queſtion;*

Cl. Aqua vivæ Induſtriæ c. 5. n. 6.

for

for otherwife the excellent virtue of Blind Obedience would fail——— and that *they muft be as a Carkafs, which fuffers it felf to be carried any way.* And which is yet nearer to the purpofe (becaufe thofe are but. particular Rules) Cardinal *Tolet* faith, *If a Country-man, concerning Arti-* Ibid. *cles of Faith, do believe his Bifhop propofing fome Heretical point, he merits by believing, although it be an Error ; becaufe he is bound to believe, till it appears to him to be againft the Church.* Bellarmine fomewhere brings it down to the Parifh-Prieft or Confeffor ; but becaufe at the prefent I can't remember the place, I fhall omit it ; but if our Author has a mind to be inftructed from us Proteftants in· their own Authors, I queftion not but to gratify him with it, and with many others of the like kind.

No Man can be a Papift, but he whofe Eyes are blinded Affert. 15. *by Education, or he who puts cut his Eyes by Atheifm.* The Preacher infers this from the former, *No Man therefore can be a Papift,* &c. Whether the latter Propofition be reafonably infer'd from the Premifes, I leave to our Author's *Faculty* to judge : But this I may fay without offence, that he that knows·not his Right hand from his Left, or needs to be taught which is his *Right*, and which is. his *Left* ; or will believe him that tells him what he knows to be his *Right*, is yet the *Left* ; or thinks himfelf bound to believe him that fo tells him, whatever·place his Teacher holds in the Church, how high foever his prerogative of Teaching be ; He that is in this condition, and that is of this mind, had need have fomething to be beholding to ; and if Education be not that, I know not what is : For to believe againft Senfe and Reafon, is one of the hardeft things in the World. And it's to be fear'd· the Church that obliges its Members fo to do, had need to keep men much in the dark, and to tye them up very

E hard,

hard, or elfe that they will be of no Religion, whilft they are for that Religion, which allows them not to know what they know.

Affert. 16. *They pray unto Images for the Pardon of their Sins.* The Images in the Church of *Rome,* are the Reprefenters of thofe to whofe memory, and for whofe Honour and Adoration they are Confecrated and fet up: And fo what Honour is due to the Reprefented, is exhibited to the Reprefenter; and he that proftrates himfelf before them,. and there Addreffes and leaves his Prayers, is fuppofed to proftrate himfelf before, and addrefs his Prayers to, and leave them with the Holy perfons thereby Reprefented; who are the more pleafed and the better accept them for this Honour done to themfelves by their Images. And therefore he that thus worfhips, and thus prays, thus worfhips and thus prays to the Image, as to the perfon he would thus worfhip, and thus pray to, if he was vifibly prefent; and how nicely foever men may fpeak in difputation, yet if we will take it from St. *Auguftin,* he faith,

Epift. 49. *That none can pray or adore, beholding an Image, who is not fo affected, and doth not think that he is heard by it.* Now whether this is not likely to be fo, I fhall detain the Reader with a fhort Story, ferioufly told by *Cornelius*

De Clavis Dominicis, c. 5. p. 61. *Curtius.* There is an Image of Chrift at Lucca (of which he gives the Sculpture) *which had Silver Shoes, before which a poor man proftrated himfelf, and prayed Chrift to help him in his great neceffity.* At his Prayers the Image, Aut potius Chriftus in Imagine, or rather Chrift in the Image, *bowed himfelf, and offered his Right Shoe to the Beggar, which he took; but it was redeemed by the Church, tho' it could never be put upon the foot again.* Now what could the poor Man think, and what doth *Curtius* think, but that Chrift was there prefent in the Image? and to what image would the Suppliant then repair, or where

could

could he think to be so well heard for the future as there? And why should he not pray to that Image, which thus effectually answered his Prayers, and shew'd by its Actions that he might commendably pray to it? And if they may, and do pray to Images, why not for pardon of Sins? For of whom they are heard, by them they may obtain pardon; according to the quality of the Persons thereby represented: And if they may say to the Cross, *thou our only Hope*, they may pray again, *blot out the Sins of the Guilty.* Of this see Assertion 8.

This is one of the *Absolute Falsities*, and *Wicked Calumnies*, the Adviser charges upon the Pulpits; There it's preached, *they pray to Images for the pardon of their Sins.* And without doubt he hoped the Reader would take it for such upon his credit without further examination. Whether, if it had been preached, it was a *Falsity*, let what has been said be consider'd. But what if this was not said by the Preacher? Where then will lie the *Falsity* and *Calumny*? For that let the Adviser answer if it be proved upon him, and let me answer if I do not prove it. What saith the Adviser, It was deliver'd in the Pulpit, that *they* [of the Church of *Rome*] *pray unto them* Good Advice, p. 42. (*Images*) *not only for temporal or ordinary Blessings, but for spiritual and supernatural, such as the pardon of their Sins.* I at first wonder'd why our Author placed here a full stop, and did not go along with the Preacher, who adds to *the pardon of their Sins——and the Holy Spirit, and Eternal Life.* For if the Preacher spoke this of Images, the further he had gone, the more would it have served the Adviser's purpose, to have shew'd the Absurdity of the Preacher, and the *Abuse* he puts upon them; as thus, *they pray to Images for the pardon of Sins, and the Holy Spirit, and Eternal Life.*

But he had another deſign in his eye, he thought this would look a little too groſs, the Reader might perhaps be tempted to ſee with his own Eyes. How, charge them with *praying to Images, for the Holy Spirit, and Eternal Life,* when we are told of late they pray not at all to them! And if the Reader had ſo done, he would have diſcovered the Art (I would be willing to call it the miſtake) of the Adviſer that applies that to Images, which the Preacher ſpeaks of Saints and Angels.

Let the Sermon ſpeak for it ſelf. At Page 13. the Preacher thus enters upon a new Paragraph. *What ſay you to the Doctrine of Image-worſhip ? with which I will join that other of praying to Saints and Angels.* He then begins with the firſt of theſe, and ſhews what the Council of *Trent* decreed concerning Images, what is to be underſtood by the Veneration decreed therein to be given to them, and what is the practice of their Church. Of this part he diſcourſes for near a Page together. Having finiſhed this, he proceeds to the ſecond Branch, *viz.* Invocation of Saints and Angels, in theſe words.

And they do all the external Honour to the Saints and Angels in the Addreſſes they make unto them, whether immediately, or as Repreſented by Images, that 'tis imaginable they ſhould do to our Saviour himſelf, or the Bleſſed Trinity.

Nay, they pray unto them not only for Temporal or Ordinary Bleſſings, but for Spiritual and Supernatural, ſuch as the pardon of their Sins, and the Holy Spirit, and Eternal Life. So that till our Author can make Images and Saints to be the ſame, he muſt be contented with his own words, that it's an *Abſolute Falſification.* And it did concern him therefore with a gentle ſcore -- to bring one Paſſage from the beginning of the firſt Branch to the laſt of the ſecond Branch, and to place them together, the

better

better to cover the *Abuse* he puts upon the Preacher and
Reader together.

The Paſſion of Chriſt takes away only the Guilt of Mortal Aſſert. 17.
Sins, not their Eternal Puniſhment.

This Aſſertion implies theſe things.

1. That the Guilt of Sin may be taken away, when
the Puniſhment is not

2. That the Guilt is taken away by one cauſe, *viz.*
the Paſſion of Chriſt, and the Eternal Puniſhment by
another.

3. That the Paſſion of Chriſt only takes away the
Guilt of Mortal Sins, but doth not take away the Eternal Puniſhment.

1. The firſt of theſe is granted, being one of the main
Principles the Doctrine of Purgatory depends upon. So
the Council of *Trent, Seſſ. 6. c. 14. Seſſ. 14. c. 12.*

2. They grant that the Guilt is pardoned for one reaſon, and the Puniſhment taken away for another.

So *Bellarmine* ſaith of the firſt, *All Divines teach that* De pœnit. l. 4.
Satisfaction is not offered to God, nor exacted from men for c. 1. SS. Jam
the Fault, for God doth diſcharge us from the Fault by his igitur cum.
Grace. And yet he hath a whole Chapter to prove that
men may ſatisfy for the expiating that Puniſhment which cap. 3.
ſometimes remains after the remiſſion of the Fault. So that
he ſaith the Grace of God, and elſewhere the Paſſion of
Chriſt, takes away the Fault ; and the Satisfaction a man
makes, takes away the Puniſhment *truly and properly*, Ibid. c. 7. SS.
as he elſewhere ſaith. Nos igitur.

3. From hence it follows, that if the Grace of God
takes only away the fault, and that We properly ſatisfy
for the puniſhment, that ſo far as the puniſhment is taken
away by our ſatisfactions, ſo far it is not taken away by
the Merit of Chriſt. And therefore how far ſoever the
Grace of God, and Merit of Chriſt may be otherwiſe
con-

concerned, yet there is, as to the punishment, a pecu-
liarity ascribed to Human Satisfactions. Thus *Bellar-*
mine, *It doth seem the most probable, that there is but*
one actual Satisfaction, and that is ours.

4. This is granted of Temporal Punishment, that it's
not taken necessarily away with the Guilt, but that the
Punishment may remain after the Guilt is pardoned:
but the Question will rest upon the Eternal Punishment.

For the understanding of which, it's to be remembred,
that they teach that the punishment due to Sin is not
properly removed with the Guilt, but that in kind it remains after the remission of it. This *Bellarmine* agrees
to in the words of *Cajetan* ; Cardinal *Cajetan rightly ex-*
plains this, viz. *That Punishment which remains to be paid*
after the Remission of the Fault, is the very same Punish-
ment of sense which the Sinner ought to have suffered in
Hell, the Eternity only being removed. So that the Punishment remains in nature the same, but is by some
means changed from Eternal into Temporal. The solu-
tion of which, when, and how, and by what means this
change is made, will lead us into a right understanding
of this matter.

Bellarmine indeed saith, that *the Eternal Punishment is*
changed into temporal, when the Guilt is forgiven. But let
this Assertion be as it will; if the Eternal Punishment
is in some cases changed into Temporal by the same
means by which the Temporal is removed ; then the
Merit and Passion of Christ is in those cases no otherwise
concerned in taking away the Eternal Punishment, than
it is in taking away the Temporal. But it is granted,
that in taking away the Temporal, the Passion of Christ is
only mediately, and remotely, and improperly concerned,
and that it's taken away immediately, and properly, and
actually, by other means, such as Satisfactions, &c. and
it

it is *de Facto* fo in exchanging the Eternal into Temporal; which is done by Satisfactions, the Power of the Keys, and Indulgences. So *Vafquez* concludes as to the Former, that God's Grace fuppofed, as to Mortal Sins, *we do indeed fatisfy God for our fin.* And as to the two P. 3. D. 2. latter, the firft about the Power of the Keys, fhall be under- c. 6. n. 38. taken, *Affert.* 21. The fecond, how Eternal Punifhment is changed into Temporal by Indulgences, I fhall remit to the Appendix.

From all which it appears, what ground there is for this Affertion of the Preacher, that *the Paffion of Chrift takes away only the Guilt of Mortal Sins, not their Eternal Punifhment ;* that is, that there are thofe ways of taking away the *Eternal Punifhment* in the Church of *Rome,* and of changing it into Temporal, which do no more concern the Paffion of Chrift in it, than in taking away the Temporal ; that is properly, immediately, and actually taken away by Humane Satisfactions, &c.

The bare faying of Prayers, without minding what they Affert. 18. *fay, is acceptable to God.* The words of the Preacher are here but partially related , For thus they are produced. *What fay you to the Doctrine of* opus operatum, *which makes the meer work done in all Acts of Devotion fufficient to Divine Acceptance : particularly the bare faying of Prayers, without either minding what they fay, or underftanding it.* So that what the Advifer quotes is a particular of the foregoing General, and brought by the Preacher as an inftance of what he had charged upon them. He tells his Auditors, *that meer work done in Acts of Devotion, is,* in the opinion of the Church of *Rome, fufficient to Divine Acceptance.* To this our Author hath nothing, it feems, to fay, and indeed it's fo agreeable to the Council of *Trent,* that he that will deny it, is in danger of its *Ana-* Sep. 7. Can. *thema.* But fuppofing any one fhould be fo hardy as to 8. 12.

deny

deny it; the Preacher fortifies it with an Inſtance, *Meer Acts of Devotion are*, ſaith he, *ſufficient*; for ſo is *the bare ſaying of Prayers, without either minding what they ſay, or underſtanding it.* And yet leſt this ſhould want of its force, he goes on: *And agreeably hereunto the Romiſh Church enjoins the ſaying of them in a Language unknown to the generality of her Children.* If I am not miſtaken, our Author has here involved himſelf in no ſmall difficulty, and muſt either grant that which he would faſten as a *Falſification* upon the Preacher; or (which is worſe) muſt condemn his own Church for enjoyning the Worſhip of God to be ſo adminiſtred, as to be unacceptable to him. It's apparent that the Publick Prayers in their Church are in a Language unknown to the Generality of the People; it's as Evident, that they cannot mind what they do not know nor underſtand; and he acknowledges here, that without minding what they ſay, their Prayers are not acceptable to God. So that conſequently Prayers in an Unknown Tongue, are not acceptable to God. I know our Author is no friend to Inferences; and it's likely he will put the caſe upon another iſſue, that the Preacher charged this as a Doctrine of the Church of *Rome*, that *the bare ſaying of Prayers, without minding what they ſay, is acceptable to God.*

And it's likely there he will ſtick, unleſs he conceals himſelf under the words, *minding what they ſay*: I was upon this running to Cardinal *Tolet*, to *Salmeron*, &c. to give our Author ſatisfaction in the point; but I conſidered that was a great way to go, and a good ſubſtantial Engliſh Author might do as well: and to him I recommend ours; and that is the Repreſenter, who ſaith:

Pap. Miſrepr. and Repr. ch. 25. *It's an undeniable thing, that, to ſay Prayers well and devoutly, 'tis not neceſſary to have attention on the words, or on the ſenſe of the Prayers.* And having brought theſe two

Friends

Friends together, I leave them to compound the matter between them; and shall pass on.

They appear before God in their Churches Dumb and Senseless, like an Idol. The Adviser had done the Preacher more right, if he had kept to his words, *So are the People to appear before God*, &c. For the *So* would have intimated the Connexion they have to somewhat foregoing; and the words, *the People*, would have shew'd that the Clergy were not herein included (though many of them are involved in the same case, if their own Authors are to be credited.) To return, the Preacher saith, *The Pope takes from them the knowledge of the Prayers offer'd in their name, and lets them not understand their own desires. So are the People to appear before God dumb and senseless like one of their Idols.* Now here it's suppos'd that all publick Prayers are offer'd up to God in the name of the People; that the People ought to know what is put up in their name, and to join in it, that by their consent they may be Their prayers and desires : and that if they do not understand, nor give their Amen and Consent (which they cannot do unless they understand) that then they are *dumb* and *senseless*; by which means their Prayers are defeated of their Acceptance, and they of their Right. Now I would fain understand, what is the part of the People, and wherein they are concerned; if not in what is done for them, and in their behalf; or for what end even their Service is so compos'd; as to have in it Petitions, Exhortations to attention, Responses, Lessons, Creeds, &c. which in the first design of them were contrived and ordered for the People, and in the nature of them do imply it; and yet the People too be as *dumb* to speak, and as *senseless* to understand as an Idol? The matter of Fact, that so it is, is evident against our Adviser's Remark; but the Reason of it I am yet to understand.

F   *They*

Asser. 19.

Sixt. Senenf. Biblioth. l. 6. Annot. 263.

Aſſert. 20.

· *They avowedly allow what God poſitively forbids.* The words of the Preacher, as afore-recited, are, *They abſolve in ſome caſes from the obedience of God himſelf, and avowedly allow, what he as poſitively forbids ; authorize Inceſtuous Conjunctions, and licenſe Perjury.* The Charge has two Branches, *viz.* the abſolving from what God commands, and the allowing what he forbids ; but though theſe are oppoſite Terms, yet as the Authority of God is equally concerned in both, ſo it's equally invaded in the violation of either. And whether the Church of *Rome* forbids what God commands, or allows what he forbids, She is (if guilty) equally an Offender. And that remains to be tried, in which I ſhall follow our Author, and confine my ſelf to his branch, *they allow what God forbids.*

It is a ſaying of Cardinal *Zabarel*, that in the Church of *Rome*, *they have perſuaded the Popes that they might do all things whatſcever they pleaſed, although unlawful* ; and that, *ſint, pluſquam Deus, more than God.*

But this however true, may ſeem to be too extravagant ; and it's more than I am obliged to prove. But let us ſee what power is challenged, and then we ſhall find

De Conceſſ.
præbend. è
propoſuit, &c.

    1. The Canoniſts agreeing that there is no Divine Law but what the Pope may diſpence with, except the Articles of Faith.

Cont. Cajet. 6.
p. 524.

    2. Wherein any of the Divines do differ from the Canoniſts, it is not in the power, but the way of explaining

De vot. 1. 6.
c. 9. n. 7. &c.

it, ſaith *Catharinus,* whether it be properly or improperly : that is, ſaith *Suarez,* it's no formal Diſpenſation of the Divine Law but the matter of the Law is changed.

    3. The ſame Author ſaith, It's manifeſt the Church hath granted real Diſpenſations in this kind ; and the Gloſs upon the Canon-Law gives us ſome Inſtances, in which the Pope doth diſpence againſt the Law of God, as *Vows* and *Oaths.*

†

Of

Of the Former *Escobar* faith, that by virtue of a Bull the Vow of not finning may be changed, as in Fornication. Theol. Mor. To. 1. l. 7. c. 20. n. 23.

Of the Latter, *viz.* Difpenfing with Oaths, the Inftances are fo notorious and many, and fo often produced, that it need not to be infifted upon. After all it muft be confefs'd, that the Preacher fail'd in the modifh way of expreffing himfelf; for he fhould have faid, the Church hath a Power of *altering* the Nature of things, and that what was before an *Inceftuous Conjunction,* is by the Difpenfation made lawful and honeft, and not inceftuous; and then it's likely our Advifer might have had nothing to fay. It's no matter whether we cannot find out the difference, when they do.

To Confefs, and to be Abfolved, is fufficient for the Forgivenefs of Sins, though there be no Sorrow for the Sins at all, but only for the Penance. It is fo, faith the Preacher, *in effect*; when, *It is not neceffary to this Abfolution, that they fhould be contrite or heartily forry; for Attrition with Auricular Confeffion, fhall pafs inftead of Contrition.* I am here at a ftand, to know whether our Author objects againft the Doctrine the Preacher charges upon the Church of *Rome*; or againft what he faith, it is *in effect.* Methinks there is little Reafon for the Latter; for if Forgivenefs of Sins be the confequence of a juft Abfolution, and if that be a juft Abfolution which is the confequent of Confeffion and Attrition, then certainly *to Confefs, and to be Abfolved, is fufficient for the Forgivenefs of Sins, though there be no forrow for the Sins at all, but only for the Penance,* that is, though there be only Attrition; for what is Attrition, but a forrow for the penance and the punifhment threatned to Sin, though there be no true forrow for the Sin? So that the Point will reft upon the Former, *Whether Attrition with Confeffion doth pafs* Affert. 25. Concil. Trid. Seff. 14. c. 4.

F 2 *inftead*

inftead of Contrition ? This I confefs the Council of *Trent*
is cautious in, becaufe it's a Doctrine fo manifeftly re-
pugnant to the Scripture, and gives fo great a liberty to
fin, that it's highly fcandalous; but yet it takes care to
fecure the Reputation of their Church in a matter of
greater confequence to them, and that is, Infallibility,
and that it doth by covertly maintaining this Doctrine
which had been long a prevailing Doctrine in their
Church.   For firft, we are there told, that *the Sacraments do confer grace upon all, and always upon fuch as
rightly receive them.* And again, that *Attrition doth difpofe the Sinner to receive the grace of God in the Sacrament
of Penance— and doth bring to Juftification.* Now if Attrition doth difpofe the Sinner for Juftification, and for
the Grace of God in that Sacrament, and the Sacraments do confer Grace on thofe that are difpofed; then
the Grace of God is received, and the Sinner juftified
upon Attrition, though without Contrition.

This is more fully exprefs'd in the Catechifm, which
faith, *Though the Sinner be not affected with fuch a grief for
his fin, as may be fufficient for pardon; yet when he has
rightly confefs'd to a Prieft, all his Sins are pardoned, and
by the power of the Keys in Abfolution an entrance is opened
into Heaven.* If there was need for it, I could multiply
Authorities from the Cafuifts (who certainly are proper
Teftificators to it) but I fhall appeal for it to the privi-
lege obtained (as it's faid) by the Bleffed Virgin for her
devoted Clients, which is, that *none of them can depart
this life without Sacramental Confeffion,* and all Grace be-
longing to it: of which I fhall give a remarkable Inftance.   " A certain Bandito having underftood from a
" poor Woman, and fhe from a Holy Man *in the Pulpit,*
" that whoever fafted upon the Saturday, in Devotion to
" the Bleffed Virgin, fhould be fure to Confefs in the
                                                        " point

Seff. 7. de Sa-
cram. Can. 6.
Seff. 14. cap 4.

Cat. ad Pa-
roch. par. 2.
c. 5. SS. 38.

" point of Death, nor fhould depart without true Pe-
" nance, and fhould avoid Damnation. He vowed to
" obferve this as long as he lived, which he did; but
" after many years it happened this Robber was furpri-
" zed in his Wickednefs. and without delay had his
" Head ftruck off Which was no fooner done, but the
" Head thus fevered from the Body, cried out *Confeffion*,
" *Confeffion, Con'effion*. The Standers by amazed, fent
" for a Prieft to the next Village, who laying the Head
" to the Body, The Thief told them that he had this
" grace fhewed him, becaufe he had done this good in
" his life, that he fafted on the Saturday; and that when
" the Devils would have taken away his Soul, the Blef-
" fed Virgin appeard, and would not permit the Soul to
" go out of the Body, till he was fully contrite, and had
" confefs'd all his Sins. Which having done, he died.

I have indeed the Story immediately from *Spinellus*, Pet. Spinelli Amor Dei pa-
(and who will may find more there of the fame kind) ræ Virginis.
but he from *Pelhartus*, and *Anfelm*, and the Book called Colon. 1649.
Scala Cœli : and *Spinellus*'s Book is licenfed by the Gene- cap. 1. n. 24.
ral of the Jefuits, *Cl. Aqua Viva*, &c. There was a time
it feems when this Doctrine was taught in the Pulpits,
and it's ftill good Doctrine with others; and whether we
muft take this Doctrine of the Church from thofe, or the
Advifer, needs no great deliberation.

An Indulgence or Pope's Pardon purchas'd with Money, Affert. 22.
ferves with them inftead of Sanctification, and a Godly Life.
The Indulgences are (as the Preacher faith well enough)
the *merits of others ftored up in the Churches Treafury,* and
diftributed according as the chief Steward of it fees fit, V. Pope Cle-
and upon what terms he pleafes to thofe that have them ment. VI. in Conftit. in
not of their own. The Preacher faith it is *by way of Com-* Bellarm. de In-
mutation inftead of Holinefs, and a Godly Life, for thofe dulg. l. 1. c. 2,
who give Money for them. The Firft of thefe he wanted SS. ult.

not

not Authority for; for by thofe were Perfons of the moft profligate Lives encouraged to go for the Holy Land, and on other Expeditions, when they had thereby indulged, and had a promife of an Eternal Reward; though guilty of thofe Sins that excluded out of the Kingdom of Heaven, as the Hiftorians tell us: and which were fo abfolute and plenary upon other occafions in future Ages, that it encouraged the Diffolute, and became offenfive to the Virtuous. So *Conradus Urfpergenfis* faith, *That by plenary Indulgences more Wickednefs was brought into the World; and that they faid, Let me act what Wickednefs I will, I fhall by thefe be deliver'd from Punifhment:* So *Polydore Virgil* faith, *That after Indulgences were grown common, many did lefs abftain from Evil Actions.* So the *Centum Gravamina, n. 3. An. 1523.*

Gul. Tyrius Hiftor. Orient.

Chron. p. 322.

De Invent. l. 8. c. 1.

And ftill the cafe grew worfe, and the Scandal increafed, as thefe were expofed to Sale; and thofe that had no mind to perform the Penance, or obferve other Conditions, might buy it off with Money: By which means, though *Rome* grew rich, yet the Ecclefiaftical Authority was brought into contempt, and encouragement was given to many Sins; as their own Hiftorians do obferve. And this (as it's well known) gave the occafion to the Reformation in *Germany*, when *Leo* the Xth proftituted the Indulgences to all Comers, and his Bankers promifed pardon without any diftinction of time, place or fin, as an Hiftorian obferves. See more of this in the Appendix.

Urfperg. Chron. p. 307. Platina in Bonif. 9.

Auricular Confeffion is the means whereby the Clergy work their Plots and Projects; 'tis a matter of meer Intereft; and were there no gain in it, their chief Champions would be afhamed of it. The words of the Preacher are, *Auricular Confeffion their great Intelligencer, the main curb of the Laity, whereby the Clergy hold them in awe, in being admitted*

Affert. 23.

admitted to all the Secrets of States and Families, thereby to work their Purpofes, their Plots, &c.

Now by this we are led to difcover,

1. What Confeffion is, and how fit a means fuch a fort of Confeffion is to let them into the knowledg of Secrets.

2. What ufe has been made of it in their Church.

1. Confeffion in the Church of *Rome* requires " be- fore-hand a diligent Premeditation, and Examination " of the Confcience about all and fingular Mortal Sins, " even the moft fecret, whether Acts, Thoughts, or De- " fires, with all their Aggravations, and Circumftances, " fo far as may change the nature of the Sin, and then " to difcover all thofe that they can call to mind, to the " Prieft, from whom they expect Abfolution. This Con- " feffion they fay is neceffary to all after Baptifm *Jure* " *Divino* ; and if any Perfon knowingly retain any of " thefe from the knowledg of his Confeffor, he can have " no benefit of the Abfolution.

Concil. Trid. Seff. 14. c. 5. Can. 6, 7.

By this means, I hope, the firft part of the Preacher's Charge is fufficiently evident. For if the moft fecret thoughts of that kind are to be laid open before the Con- feffor, and none of the Mortal Sins, nor their circum- ftances that affect the kind and nature of them, are to be omitted, certainly the Fathers muft be let thereby into, if not all, yet the greateft *Secrets of States and Families, and hold them in awe* ; for if at any time their Penitents do ftep afide, and give them any provocation, or elfe refufe to act according to their Injunction, they are at their mercy whether they fhall profper, or be ruined in this World ; or whether they fhall ftand abfolved or con- demned as to another. So that if the Confeffors have a mind to *work their Purpofes, their Plots and Projects*, there cannot be a more ufeful Expedient than this. For what

may

may not they do who have the Consciences, the Reputation, the Safety here, and Salvation of men hereafter in their power ? And if any thing under Heaven will support the *Romish* Church, this will. So that it is of the greatest consequence to maintain it, and to stamp a *Jus Divinum* upon it, to make it a Sacrament, and denounce an *Anathema* against them that shall call it into question. Therefore the Preacher thought he had reason to say, *should that go down, then farewell Popery.*

2. The next thing is to enquire into the matter of Fact, and to see whether what lies so fair for such an end has not been applied to it, and made to serve it. And of this among many I shall only give an Instance or two. The Story of the Holy League in *France* is well known to the World, and though not made more truly known, is made more famous, by the History of it not long since published by *Lewis Maimbourg.* In that League we are told by a much better and more faithful Historian,

Hist. I. 85. Leydæ 1646. p. 100.
the great *Thuanus,* That the Confessors in private Confessions did calumniate the King; and did not only maintain it lawful for Subjects to enter into Leagues against his Consent, but that they sometimes refus'd to absolve their Penitents without they would join in the Design then on foot against *Henry* the IIId. The same use was made of this Divine Institution (as they would have it) by Father *Arnold,* Confessor to *Lewis* the XIIIth of *France,*

Memoires de Duæ de Rohan. lib. 1.
who made the King to swear solemnly at Confession never to intermeddle with Affairs of State, nor to controul or dislike the Measures and Proceedings of the then powerful Favourite and great Minister of State, *Luines.* Now the Question is, whether our Author himself be not *ashamed* of such practices ; and if he be, and the whole Church has the same reason for it, what then is the Reason, for which it was tied so strictly upon the

Con-

Consciences of men thus to confess, and all must be damn'd (as far as the Church can damn them) that put not themselves into the power of their Confessors.

They are bound to vow Ignorance under the severest Pe- Assert. 24. *nalties.* The words of the R. R. Preacher are——*Ignorance the Mother of their Devotion, which they are bound to by Vow, and under the severest Penalties ; so that it is a Mortal Sin, so much as to doubt of any part of their Religion.*

That Ignorance is the Mother of Devotion, is one of their known Maxims ; and this without doubt was one reason why some of the most Devout among them, such as St. Benedict, St. Francis, and *Ignatius Loyola*, were also some of the most Ignorant : And if the Observation be true, there is the same reason for encouraging Ignorance in the Vulgar, and obliging others to it in many cases, as there is for encouraging Devotion, which is, it seems, the Daughter of it. From hence I conceive it was, that St. *Benedict*, in the Rules given to those of his Order, obliges them to such a course of Devotion as will secure them against what he himself was a hater of, Humane Learning ; and that herein they might be like to their Founder, of whom St. *Gregory* saith, he was *knowingly ignorant, and wisely unlearned.* So that he that Dial. lib. 2. vows to observe these Rules, vows to be ignorant ; and if he be knowing and learned otherwise than he is devout, he must either break his Vow to obtain it, or must acquire it more by Inspiration than Industry, which the strictness of his Rule will not afford him sufficient leisure for. This they *are bound to by Vow*, as the Preacher saith ; but that any among them are *bound to vow Ignorance*, as the Adviser makes the Preacher to say, that I know no more than the Preacher saith it. To be bound to it *by Vow*, is to say this Vow binds to it ; but to be

G bound

bound *to vow*, is to to be bound before the Vow. To this the next Aſſertion is a-kin.

Aſſert. 25.

Their avowed Principles are to keep the People in ignorance. For proof of this, let us review what is charged upon them by theſe Preachers. As,

1. *That Ignorance is with them the Mother of Devotion.* So we are told, that *ſuch as pray in Latin, though they underſtand not what they ſay, do pray with as great devotion, and oftentimes more than others that pray in a Tongue they underſtand :* and that *no underſtanding of words can be compared to it.* So that if they *do keep the People in ignorance,* they act but conformable to this Principle.

Rhem. Annot. in 1 Cor. 14. p. 452.

Card. Hoſius de ling. Vernac.

2. The Preacher ſaith (which the Adviſer hath cautiouſly left out) *If you do but blindly believe as the Church believes, and blindly obey what is impoſed upon you, you are good Catholicks.* And what is this, if true, but an encouragement to be ignorant ? And that it's true, I have ſhew'd Aſſertion 14, and 15. And ſo *Bellarmine* tells us, that the People are to reſt ſatisfied *in the Judgment of their Superiors.* And ſay the Rhemiſts, *He ſaith enough, and defendeth himſelf ſufficiently, that anſwereth he is a Catholick man, and will live and die in that Faith,* &c. *and that his Church can give a reaſon of all things which they demand of him.*

Dr. S's Serm. p. 28.

De Juſtif. l. 1. c. 7.

Annot. in Luk. 12. 11.

3. The Preacher ſaith, *It is a Mortal Sin ſo much as to doubt of any part of their Religion.* Which is in other words what is ſaid by *Navar,* &c. that *it's an Hereſie* (and ſure that's a Mortal Sin) *to diſpute a point of Faith,* and he incurs the ſupicion of it that doth but queſtion it. And to ſecure from doubting, an Heretick (as they call him) when reclaim'd to their Church, is to ſwear with an Imprecation to continue in it; with which Doubting is not very well conſiſtent.

Manual. c. 11. n. 26.

Pontificale.

4. They

4. They take away *the Key of Knowledg*, the Holy Scriptures, and forbid the People to have or read them *under the greatest Penalties.* And the time has been, that those Parents have been brought to the Stake, that taught their Children so much as the Lord's Prayer, the ten Commandments, and the Apostles Creed, in the Vulgar Tongue. Burn. Hist. of the Reformat. par.1. l.1.p.31.

Now if all this be not *to keep the People in Ignorance*, nothing is: And if it be not their *avowed Principle* to keep them so, it's not easy to know what is.

They teach their People better Manners, than to rely upon the all-sufficient Merits of Christ. The Preacher here supposes, that since the Merits of Christ are All-sufficient, there is no need of the Merits of others; and that we cannot rely on our own Merits, or the Merits of others, without derogating from the All-sufficient Merits of Christ. For the better understanding of the Case, and Vindication of the Preacher in this matter, Proposit. 26.

1. I shall observe, That the Church of *Rome* teaches, that we both can and do merit by Good Works. Thus the Council of *Trent* maintains, That *the Good Works of justified Persons are not so the gifts of God, but that they are also the Merits of the justified, and do truly Merit an increase of Grace here, and Glory hereafter.* And that as *Bellarmin* saith, *Because of the Work it self, altho there were no Covenant or Promise from God.* And as *Vasquez* adds, without the merits of Christ. For thus he states the Point, *There is no increase of value accrues to the Works of just Men by the Merits or Person of Christ, which they would not have had otherwise freely confer'd upon them from the same Grace by God alone, without Christ.* And he afterwards infers, That supposing the Merits of Christ to have obtained Grace for us to work, *We have no more* Sess.6. Can.32. De Justif. l. 5. c. 17, &c. In 1a, 2dæ, q. 114. d. 214. c. 7. Art. 8. d. 222. c. 3. n. 30,31.

need

need of Chriſt's Merits to ſupply our defects, but that our own Good Works are of themſelves ſufficient. Now, if they thus teach that Good Works do truly merit, and that tho there were no Promiſe of God, and *without Chriſt;* I leave it to every one to judg whether they do not teach the People to rely on ſomewhat elſe than the Merits of Chriſt.

2. They teach the People to rely on the Merits of others. As.

1. In their Doctrines of Supererogation and Indulgences; the former of which, is the Overplus of the Satisfactions of the Saints, as well as of Chriſt, depoſited in the common Stock or Treaſury of the Church. The later is the diſpenſing, iſſuing out, and applying that Stock, as the great Conſervator of it, the Pope, ſees meet; and by Virtue of which the defect of Merit in others is by that means compenſated.

2. They teach the People alſo, to rely on the Merits of others in their Doctrine of the Invocation of Saints and Angels, whereby they conſtitute other Mediators than the alone Mediator Jeſus Chriſt; whom they are taught to *fly to for Aid,* and whoſe Merits they depend upon for ſucceſs in the things they are Sollicitors for.

3. They are taught this farther, when they are taught to join the Merits of the Saints, with thoſe of Chriſt in their Offices; and however they ſometimes conclude in the Name of Chriſt, yet in the Body of the Collects the Merits of the Saints are made the ground of their Hope, as, *Grant that we may be helped or delivered by the Merits of bleſſed Saturnus,* or *Andrew,* or *Nicholas, &c.* If I ſhould tax their Forms of Invocation to the Virgin *Mary,* I might compoſe a Treatiſe of it, where they are taught to recommend all their Hope and Comfort to her, and to deſire that through her Merits and Interceſſion all may be directed, *&c.*   So

So that if to direct them to the Merits of others, to rely on them, to make them the ground of their hopes, to plead what they have done as an argument for their own fuccefs, and to pray to them as thofe that have merited to be heard ,for others, be to teach their people to rely on fomewhat elfe than the Merits of Chrift, then the Preacher was not out in afcribing this Doctrine to them.

But yet at laft the way of wording it, may feem liable to exception, *viz. They teach the people better manners than to rely*, &c. But in this the Preacher is not fo much to be blamed, fince he herein manifeftly alludes to the Argument they ufe for the Interceffion of Saints and Angels, and their Invocation of them, which I fhall chufe to deliver in the words of one of their own Authors: *After the Pater Nofter, it is to be* observed that the ufual cuftom of the Catholick Church is to *second it with an Ave Mary, whereby we do imitate the beft* manner of folliciting with a temporal Prince, to whom having *humbly delivered our Petition, for more affurance of better* fuccefs, we make alfo recourfe to fome powerful Favourite,&c. Poor man's Devotion Par. 167. p. 477. Now if Chrifts Merits be all-fufficient, and what we are taught folely to rely upon, then their Courtly Argument of other Favourites and Interceffors and Merits, however mannerly it may be in conceit, is an affront to the Merits of our Saviour; and fo much the more as a fufficiency in any refpect is given to theirs, is there a derogation from the All-fufficiency of His.

The Clergy muft live a fingle Life, whether honeftly or no, it makes no matter. Affert. 27.

The reafon why they muft live fingly, is for fear left having Wives and Children, they fhould give the State fecurity of their Obedience to their Soveraign. Affert. 28.

In thefe two Affertions of the Preacher, there are thefe Three Things contained,

1. That

1. That the Clergy in the Church of *Rome*, muſt and are obliged by the order of the Church, and their own Vow, to lead a ſingle life.

2. That there is more care taken that they live *ſingly*, than that they live *honeſtly*.

3. That there are Political Reaſons for this Impoſition, of which the *giving the State ſecurity* is one.

1. The firſt is determined by the Firſt and Second Councils of *Lateran*, &c. and is out of diſpute.

2. That there is more care taken that the Clergy live ſingle, than that they live honeſtly; I think is undeniable, if we may judg of it by the Puniſhments, the Allowances, and Reſolutions of the Caſe.

As to the Puniſhments, if a Clergy-man be found to be married, he muſt either be ſeparated from his Wife, or be deprived : So it has been decreed, and ſo it was executed in the Reign of Queen *Mary*; but if one in Orders keeps a Concubine, the Pope's *Taxa* fines him but 7 *Groſſes*, or about 10 *s.*

Thuanus Tom. 1. An. 1553. Tax. Camer. Apoſt.

As to the Allowances, one is abſolutely forbidden, without any relaxation or Diſpenſation, the other has been openly allowed and licenſed upon a Yearly Penſion, as *Eſpencæus* complains.

In Tit. c. 1. Digreſ. 1.

And if we come to compare caſe with caſe, it's reſolved, that the one is a ſin greater than the other; ſo *Coſterus* the Jeſuit ; *If a Prieſt commits Fornication, or keeps a Concubine at home, altho he is guilty of a grievous Sacriledg, yet he ſins more grievonſly if he marries.*

Enchir de. Cœlib. c. 15.

3. That there are Political Reaſons for this Impoſition, and continuing it. It's granted by many learned men of that Church (ſuch as Cardinal *Cajetan* and *Antoninus,*&c.) That the Marriage of Prieſts is not forbidden by any Divine, but by the Eccleſiaſtical Law, and ſo may be, and has been in ſeveral Caſes diſpenſed with by the Pope.

†

It

It has been obferved and lamented by feveral pious Perfons among them, that the Celibacy of Priefts has produced grievous Enormities, and that however ufeful it might have been in fome feafon, yet now being turned to the contrary, that the Church ought to do as a good Phyfitian, that when he finds his Medicines rather hinder than promote the Cure, lays them afide. So the Prudent *Caffander*, and Pope *Pius* the IId.

Confult. Art. 23. Platina.

Now when this is the Cafe, and the Church fuffers fo much by the Scandal, and the Souls of many by the indifpenfable obligation to Celibacy, why it fhould not be in thefe circumftances relaxed, I know not of any other reafons imaginable, than what are Political.

It's given as one reafon by *Gerfon* and *Bonaventure*, why Marriage was not forbidden to the Clergy in the Primitive Church, becaufe it did not then abound in wealth and poffeffions as now : And we may hereby guefs for what reafon it is now forbidden, and that is, that the Treafure acquir'd by the Church may not be diverted, and that all within it having no other Relations than the Church, their care and endeavour may be directed thither, and their whole dependance may be upon it. Wife and Children are Hoftages where ever they are, and the beft Security a Prince can have from his Subjects; and whatever reafons they would find to break with him, thefe are the moft likely means to retain them in their obedience ; and therefore if the Prince has thefe in poffeffion, it will be hard for the Church whatever ufe fhe has for its Clergy, to prevail with them to venture the lofs of thefe pledges to ferve it. So that a Church that fteers it felf by Political Maxims, and hath frequent Controverfies with Crowned Heads, may fee there is reafon, if it would preferve the Clergy intire to it felf, to prevent their Engagements in fuch a ftate of life, as would rob the Mitre

of.

of ſo choice a Jewel, and tranſlate it to, and ſettle it upon the Diadem of the Prince.

Thus have I gone through theſe 28 Obſervations the Adviſer has drawn from the Sermons he quotes ; and now I will venture to leave it to the Reader's candor to judg concerning the truth of his Aſſertion in the cloſe of them, *viz*. *'Tis certain the Papiſts diſown theſe Doctrines, and preach againſt them as much as theſe very Doctors, who appear ſo zealous to condemn them.*

P. 55.

If our Author pleaſes, for the Vindication of his own Preachers, to ſhew us where they have been as zealous againſt theſe Doctrines, in their Pulpits, as thoſe he quotes and reviles have deſervedly been ; and to quote as good Authorities to clear their Church from theſe charges and imputations, as I have quoted to maintain them, he will do much better ſervice than by a riſque of Rhetorical Exclamations, try to amuſe rather than ſatisfie his Reader. He has told us, *that the moſt that can be ſaid of theſe 28 Points is, that ſome of them are miſtakes of the Preachers, others Exaggerations, others Inferences from ſome ſingle Author ; others abſolute Falſities, and wicked calumnies.* Now this would have been a work becoming himſelf to undertake, and with a gentle hand (for he muſt not preſs too hard) to have ranged theſe Points in their order, and to have told us which he would be pleaſed to leave to theſe Preachers, and which they will take to themſelves. For if he leaves it to the Preachers; they will turn the Points upon his Church, and the *wicked Calumnies* upon himſelf. The world on this ſide the Four Seas is grown too wiſe to be any longer entertained with ſuch Eccleſiaſtical Amuſements ; it's Reaſon and Authority, cloſe Arguing, and a clear ſtating of Matters, that is expected And however *Miſrepreſentations* at one time, and *Agreements* at another, and *Cautions*

ibid.

ons and *Advices* at a third, may have their turn, and be of use in defect of better; yet they will be like *Gondomar's* Lye, that may at some time do a piece of hopeful service, but is not to be too often try'd, left it become unsuccessful and ridiculous. Our Author cannot but know that this is a way they may soon be made weary of, if the Preachers should turn Writers, and could apply their time to no better purpose; since no Church in the world lies more open than his own. The cause would not then be like a taking up an occasional Sermon, *or a single Author,* and trying tricks upon it, sometimes mangling, sometimes omitting, sometimes changing, sometimes extorting that from it which was never in it. And when all is done, *the most that can be said is, that some of them are mistakes of the* Misrepresenter's *and Advisers; others Exaggeration others Inferences from some single Author, or some Abuse in Practice; others Absolute Falsities, and Wicked Calumnies.* But they would appear with a Mass of Irrefragable Authorities, such as Popes and Councils; and the *Veterane* Army of obsolete *Missals,* and *Breviaries, Offices* and *Legends,* which tho now they would have buried in oblivion, and the Writers of the Church of *England* have been so charitable of late to them, as but sparingly to produce; yet it is an Advantage against what pretends to be an Infallible Church, and the present Writers of it amongst us, that there needs not a greater. And if they had a mind to proceed, and would make Collections of Doctrines and Principles from such Books as have come forth with uncontrouled *Imprimaturs,* there will be no end of this Labour. But thanks be to God they have better things before them, and care not to squander away their time in such Inquiries, which can be of little better use than old Romances, to shew the Ignorance and Superstition of the Times in which these

H   things

things were received with the Veneration of Gospel, and the Degeneracy of that Church that brought them into the World.

' It's a mean thing for a man of Wit (as our Author is) to play away his time in such little Undertakings. He seems to be made for better things, and it would be a matter worthy of himself to try his Talent in some of the abovesaid Points, and at once to clear their Church of the Obloquy of those Doctrines, or the Doctrines from the Error charged upon them. As for example, let him employ some of his spare Minutes about reconciling Transubstantiation to Sense and Reason, or in shewing the admirable Advantage and Edification that there is in having the Service and Scripture in an Unknown Tongue; or proving the invariable Conformity of their Church, to Scripture, Antiquity, and it self, in their Infallibility, Confession, Indulgences, Images, Pilgrimages, &c. For it will be a very hard thing to believe a Church Infallible, that has mistaken, and has neither Scripture, nor Antiquity, nor it self to plead for it self. That has Missals and Breviaries, and Legends and Authentick Scriptures in one Age, that they are ashamed of in another, and for the vindication of which, are fain at last to come from the pinnacle of Infallibility, to the humility of an *Exposition*.

Pag. 50.

He may complain till Doomsday *that our Guides have gone out of the way*, and may fill the World with *Advices* and *Cautions* against the *Poison infused into Congregations from the High Places*; but it will be to little purpose, unless he proves it as well as says it, and gives a better Testimony of his Ability and Sincerity than what has appeared in this Collection.

As to his Ability (whatever it may be in a better Cause) after all the rally against the Preachers, he ha
no

t fo much as ventured upon one Point, but has acted
all along as a meer Suppofer. As to his Sincerity, if the
leaving out Quotations, and often whole Paragraphs and
Claufes tending to the explication and confirmation of
what was taught by the Preachers ; if mangling and
altering the Words and Senfe be Certificates of it, he is
one of the moft candid and ingenuous Writers of this
Age. I fhall not trouble the Reader with a Collection
of this kind, I have here and there given a tafte as I went
along, chufing rather to expofe the Argument than the
Writer ; and that being done, to haften to an end. . .

The Two remaining Cautions refer either to the defcriptions given in fome Sermons of what is held and
practiced in the Church of *Rome*, as *Pilgrimages*, *Hair-
Shirts*, &c. *the Mafs* and *Purgatory*, or elfe to the feafon
of Preaching them. In both of which it had become
our Author firft to difclaim the Charge, or difprove the
thing, before he had blamed the Preachers. For if the
Pilgrimages, going bare-foot, Hair-Shirts, and *Whips* ufed
in the Church of *Rome* are as far from being means of
going to Heaven, as the Preacher fuppofeth, he faid not
amifs, *That they may as well expect to bring a Cart, as a
Soul to Heaven by fuch means*: And if thefe are taught to
be means when they are not, they deferve to be treated
with fome Contempt and Severity. Doubtlefs, in no
place is a ftrict obfervation of the Rules of Decency and
good Order more requifite than in the Pulpit ; but to
call fome things what they are, will be contrary to both
and intolerable in the opinion of thofe that would
have them to be that which they are not ; and who are
more willing and forward to find out the faults of others,
than to efpy, acknowledg, or vindicate their own. The
matter lay fair before our Author, and it would have been
a generous Undertaking to have faftned upon the Argument,

ment, and then he might in the Cloſe, with honour and advantage have expoſed the *Contemptuous* humour that he pretends to diſcover in thoſe Preachers.

He may be pleaſed to remember *A Vindication of a Paſſage in Dr.* Sherlock's *Sermon, Preached before the Houſe of Commons,* that yet wants an Anſwer after almoſt Three Years expectation of it; and methinks thoſe that take an occaſion ſo often of late to put us in mind of the Former, ſhould as well conſider that we have not forgotten the Latter; and if the *Adviſer* had to his Invective againſt the Sermon, tack'd a ſubſtantial Reply to the *Vindication* he would have done greater ſervice to his Church, and given greater ſatisfaction to others, than by exclaiming againſt the unſeaſonableneſs of it. When could there have been a fitter opportunity for their own Vindication from the Doctrines of Depoſition, &c. than when they had this Provocation given them, before that Honourable Aſſembly? When could it have been more ſeaſonable for them to have appeared in it, however unſeaſonable they thought it in him to preach it? If this had then been done, they had gone far toward the opening the Eye of that ſolemn Aſſembly that deſired the Dr. to print it, and the ſtopping the mouths of ſuch petulant Preachers; but when they have let the Cauſe drop, as if they were willing to have it forgotten; when there has been ſo long a ſilence, till they come forth with their late *Exaggerations,* they give us too great reaſon to believe, That all this proceeds from the weakneſs of a ſort of people, that when they find themſelves not able to encounter an Adverſary, pelt him with Reproaches.

PAge 3. l. 6. after *reſt,* r. *except the two laſt.* p. 8. l. 1. r. *Preachers.* p. 14 Marg. l. 4. r. *Diſquis.* p. 19. mar. del. lin. ult. p. 22. mar. l. 1. r. *Pelag.* p. 25. mar. l. 8. r. *Pelag.* p. 25. l. 4. r. *in Conſultation,* mar. l. 19. r. 13. p. 26. l. 26 r. *Hereticks.* p. 28. l. 3 r. *into it,* mar. l. 1. r. *In* 1. Tim. p. 30. mar. l. 5. r. *Sacred.* p. 37. mar. l. 4. r. *Seſſ.* p. 43. mar. l. 2. r. *ſipara.* p. 46. mar. l. 1. r. 86. l. 5. r. *Duc.*

www.ingramcontent.com/pod-product-compliance
Lightning Source LLC
Chambersburg PA
CBHW022030080426
42733CB00007B/793